S0-ADL-887

RESOURCE BOOKS FOR TEACHERS

series editor
ALAN MALEY

NEWSPAPERS

Peter Grundy

Educational Linguistics
Library

Oxford University Press

Oxford University Press
Walton Street, Oxford OX2 6DP

Oxford New York Toronto Madrid
Delhi Bombay Calcutta Madras Karachi
Kuala Lumpur Singapore Hong Kong Tokyo
Nairobi Dar es Salaam Cape Town
Melbourne Auckland

and associated companies in
Berlin Ibadan

Oxford and *Oxford English* are trade marks of
Oxford University Press

ISBN 0 19 437192 1

© Oxford University Press 1993

First Published 1993
Second impression 1994

All rights reserved. No part of this publication may be
reproduced, stored in a retrieval system, or transmitted, in any
form or by any means, electronic, mechanical, photocopying,
recording, or otherwise, without the prior permission of
Oxford University Press.

This book is sold subject to the condition that it shall not, by
way of trade or otherwise, be lent, re-sold, hired out, or
otherwise circulated without the publisher's prior consent in
any form of binding or cover other than that in which it is
published and without a similar condition including this
condition being imposed on the subsequent purchaser.

Set by Tradespools Ltd, Frome, Somerset, UK

Printed in Hong Kong

Photocopying

You may make photocopies of the newspaper extracts in
this book for your own use, but please note that
copyright law does not normally allow multiple copying
of published materials.

Acknowledgements

This book would not have been possible without the help of many others, particularly Zack Alassani, Bill Harris, Stan Hetherington, Richard Hondy, Tomoko Kato, A M Mango, Chitra Narshi and John Simelane, all MA in Applied Linguistics students at the University of Durham, who, together with a long-suffering group of language learners, collaborated with me during a memorable week of experimental, mixed ability language teaching which relied exclusively on newspapers. I am also grateful to successive generations of EAP students at Durham, who tolerated my enthusiasm for newspapers on socialization courses, and to the *PET* 'Britain Today' teachers at Pilgrims in 1989 who provided valuable comments on my ideas.

When this project was at an early stage, I received a long letter from John Morgan, which contained several characteristically brilliant ideas that I have since tried for myself and included in this book. I am also indebted to my colleague, Arthur Brookes, for many fruitful discussions and insightful comments, and in particular for the Appendix which he generously donated to this book.

When I first approached OUP with my ideas, Alan Maley wrote several thoughtful letters which have had a shaping role in this book, as has OUP's anonymous reader of my sample submission, which was both encouraging and corrective, and OUP's two further anonymous readers of the first draft of the book whose suggestions for improvements were gratefully received and acted on.

At OUP Anne Conybeare and Julia Sallabank worked hard to improve the manuscript and tidy up what was formerly a less exact text.

'My friend from overseas' (Introduction, page 5) and the 'colleague from overseas' (Introduction, page 10) have probably forgotten their apparently casual comments, so I will allow them the luxury of remaining anonymous.

All the faults in the book are mine.

The publishers and author would like to thank the following for their kind permission to use articles, extracts, or adaptations from copyright material. There are instances where we have been unable to trace or contact the copyright holder before our printing deadline. We apologize for this apparent negligence. If notified the publisher will be pleased to rectify any errors or omissions at the earliest opportunity.

'Chips are down for jobs' from *Meet the Press* by J. Abbott: Cambridge University Press (now out of print).

'Euromania haunts language of food' by George Brock: TT 25.5.91: © Times Newspapers Ltd. 1990/91.

'£35,000 for boy of six labelled a brat', 'He's too Cosi with my girl', and 'Return by ear mail': the *Daily Mirror*.

'Ban on migrant cheats' and 'Bible-basher': the *Sun*.

'Bible-basher': the *Daily Star*.

'Skyway robber steals half a million': © the *Daily Telegraph*.

Photograph on page 47: Sally and Richard Greenhill.

Photograph on page 87: Graham Alder.

Picture on page 48: Philippa Parkinson.

Contents

3 Working with texts

6 Personal responses

The author and series editor

Peter Grundy has taught in schools in Britain and Germany, has worked in higher education as a teacher trainer, and since 1979 has been a lecturer at the University of Durham, where he teaches applied and theoretical linguistics to undergraduates and postgraduates and English for Academic Purposes to the University's overseas students. He has had considerable experience of language teaching and teacher training on summer schools and seminars in Britain and overseas stretching back over more than twenty years. He is the author of *Writing for Study Purposes* (with Arthur Brookes) and of *Language through Literature* (with Susan Bassnett).

Alan Maley worked for The British Council from 1962 to 1988, serving as English Language Officer in Yugoslavia, Ghana, Italy, France, and China, and as Regional Representative for The British Council in South India (Madras). He is currently Director-General of the Bell Educational Trust, Cambridge. He wrote *Quartet* (with Françoise Grellet and Wim Welsing, OUP 1982), and *Literature*, in this series (with Alan Duff, OUP 1990). He has also written *Beyond Words*, *Sounds Interesting*, *Sounds Intriguing*, *Words*, *Variations on a Theme*, and *Drama Techniques in Language Learning* (all with Alan Duff), *The Mind's Eye* (with Françoise Grellet and Alan Duff), and *Learning to Listen* and *Poem into Poem* (with Sandra Moulding). He is also Series Editor for the New Perspectives and Oxford Supplementary Skills series.

Foreword

Newspapers have long provided a valuable resource for language teachers and learners alike. So much so that many published courses use real or simulated newspaper articles, and most schools (and many teachers) maintain files of articles organized thematically or on the basis of their language content. (And which of us has not been rescued from lack of preparation by the providential article culled fresh from the morning newspaper?)

Language learners find newspapers motivating because they offer interesting, relevant, topical, and varied information. Equally importantly, for many, they provide one of the more obvious keys for opening up the foreign society, its preoccupations, its habitual ways of thought, and its prejudices. For these very reasons newspaper material is among the most challenging the learner is called upon to face.

Language teachers tend to use newspapers in three ways: to develop various language competencies, including reading comprehension and grammar/vocabulary work; to focus on aspects of the target society and its culture; and to stimulate discussion of issues raised by the articles.

This book, while not neglecting any of these areas, concentrates on developing an authentic response from the learners. The activities are aimed at helping learners to read newspapers as newspapers, and to react to them as real people. (See especially Chapter 6, 'Personal responses'.) All too often the newspaper article has been treated as an object for linguistic or cultural dissection and analysis. Such practices can lead to the teacher continuing to squeeze the text dry long after the sap of genuine interest has been savoured by the learners.

One of the major problems in incorporating newspaper material in books is loss of topicality. An ephemeral medium is frozen into a kind of permanence, and is rapidly perceived as dated. This book has relatively few re-printed articles. Instead it offers a very wide range of highly creative and original activities which could be applied to almost any article or extract. In this way, it provides teachers with a valuable resource for using the articles of their own choice.

Alan Maley

Introduction

'British newspapers are something else,' as a friend from overseas said to me recently. I suppose he meant that the popular Press in Britain contains little news, preferring instead the 'human interest' story. And of course he was also being mildly critical. But it is very doubtful whether this image of the British Press as 'something else' is shared by those unfortunate language learners who have been fed on a diet of inscrutable headlines ('Left in the dark over racism', etc.), boring materials from 'quality' newspapers, and interminable 'comprehension' passages. This book champions a quite different approach to the use of newspapers in English Language Teaching, an approach which, broadly speaking, puts the learner's interests first and the newspaper materials second.

The aims of this book

The overall aim of this book is to provide a range of original, practical ideas for working with newspapers. *Original* and *practical* because that is what teachers want, and *newspapers* because when one has learnt to read a newspaper in a foreign language, one begins to feel that one has gone some way towards learning the second language successfully. The ultimate aim of the book is to give the students the confidence to buy and read English-language newspapers for themselves.

In the classroom, the aim is to get students first reading newspapers and then working with what they have found in their reading. In the activities in this book, 'reading' usually involves looking for something specific; and 'working with what they have found in their reading' may mean anything from making a collage to crossing out what is distasteful.

A second methodological aim is to get the students to teach themselves, as far as possible, by giving them authentic, involving activities to work on, usually in pairs and small groups.

A third, wider aim is to provide access to an important source of information, which also, in English-speaking countries, reflects significant cultural and political attitudes.

To sum up: Although this is a resource book in the obvious sense that it contains lots of practical, newspaper-based classroom activities, its underlying purpose is not only to provide teaching resources of this kind, but also to give students practice in the skills needed to enable them to read English-language newspapers for themselves.

Who is the book for?

This book will be useful in two language-learning contexts:

- in English-speaking countries where there is a plentiful supply of English-language newspapers and where the teacher's role is to provide access to the target culture as well as to teach the target language;
- in non-English-speaking countries, where the one or two, perhaps daily, perhaps weekly, English-language newspapers are likely to be only source of authentic, genuinely contemporary written English to which the students have easy access.

The book should also provide new ideas for two different kinds of teaching context:

- the mainstream, syllabus-based EFL classroom where activities based on written materials make an important contribution to class work and where new ideas that promote authentic reading and integrate the four skills are always welcomed;
- the relatively syllabus-free, learner-centred classes often favoured on short courses in Britain, where there is a premium on new ideas which involve students, and where the support of a newspaper text can provide the important sense that something real and substantial is being studied.

This book is therefore a source of new ideas for text-based work on long-term, syllabus-based courses. And at the same time it also shows how learner-centred ideas can be productively applied, particularly on short-term, syllabus-free courses.

Newspapers in the English language classroom

There are a number of points to make about the use of newspapers in the English language classroom. Most centre on the positive advantages newspapers have over other resources, but some also remind us of the difficulties newspaper materials can pose.

Availability

English-language newspapers are available world-wide on a daily basis. Some originate from English-speaking countries, others are locally produced. In fact, there is scarcely a country in the world that does not have an English-language newspaper. They are cheap and plentiful. This source of topical material written in authentic English is too useful and important to be omitted from the language classroom.

Variety

Newspapers contain a very wide variety of text types and an immense range of information. They are therefore a natural source of many of the varieties of written English that become increasingly important as learners progress.

The reading habit

Most educated people read newspapers regularly. Here therefore are a set of latent skills that can be transferred from the mother-tongue world to the language learning world. It is especially important that the confidence and sense of familiarity everyone feels when they pick up a paper in their own language is carried over into the English language classroom. If the students expect at the outset to be able to become familiar with the materials in front of them, they are already half-way to success. This is a strong argument for authentic rather than contrived uses of newspaper materials.

Reading for information

When we read the newspapers, we exercise skimming and scanning skills of a very high order. We typically either know what we are looking for (task-based reading) or we continue reading a particular feature for just as long as it remains interesting (reading for meaning). We exercise skills of such a high order because of the nature and variety of the text in front of us—it is difficult to think of materials more naturally suited to teaching authentic reading skills in a second language, particularly when we know that second language learners usually read slowly and often inefficiently. Here are materials that we can allow our students to use class time to read without feeling guilty about it.

Content

Because newspapers are about the outside world, their use in the classroom bridges the gap between the outside world and the classroom.

Skills integration

Most of us talk about what we read in the newspapers: we make judgements about it, and we listen to the judgements our friends have made; we read passages aloud to each other; perhaps the majority of the political and social opinions we form and that colour much of our conversation come from our reading of the newspapers. We thus integrate reading with listening and speaking to a remarkable degree and in an entirely natural, unconscious way when the stimulus is a newspaper. This suggests that newspapers ought to be seen to some degree as the incidental stimulus to a wide range of communicative, integrated activities.

The authentic response

Not only are newspapers authentic materials in themselves, but our response to what we read in them, even in a second language, is likely to be authentic and personal.

Topicality

The fact that newspapers are topical is both an advantage and a disadvantage. They are the freshest of all foods in the language classroom and at the same time those with the shortest shelf-life. Many of the ideas in this book work best for human interest rather than contemporary news stories. This makes them more involving for students and at the same time helps to overcome the topicality problem—it means that you can build up a bank of human interest stories that do not date over a longer period of time.

But because newspaper materials inevitably date quite quickly, it is very important (1) to develop a wide repertoire of activities that may be applied to whatever contemporary materials are to hand, and (2) to be able to think creatively so that when necessary it is possible to devise a particular activity for a particular text. The first chapter explores ways of developing these two skills in more detail.

Culture and society

For those learning English in an English-speaking country, newspapers are probably the best single source of information about the host culture and about the most important people in the host society. A familiarity with newspapers will also make it easier to understand radio and television programmes, just as a familiarity with radio and television programmes will also make it easier to understand the newspapers. It is very noticeable that those learners who succeed with newspapers are those who acculturate (and therefore learn) most successfully. In other words, newspapers offer a short-cut to acculturation.

Difficulty

Most learners find newspapers difficult: they are full of obscure headlines, insular references to unfamiliar cultural and sporting events and personalities, dense columns of printed text, and much that reflects negatively on the host society. It is emphatically not the job of the language teacher to provide missing cultural information; but it is important to give learners the confidence to tackle newspapers, and in particular to help them find their way around them and establish a working familiarity with their content. For this reason, many of the activities in this book allow the students to choose the text they wish to work with (and can therefore largely understand). This simple procedure minimizes what can otherwise be a negative response to texts containing unfamiliar vocabulary.

Let us pause a moment to sum up what has been said so far: newspapers are a cheap, widely available, authentic resource containing an immense variety of text types; they have a crucial role to play in developing second language reading skills; and they evoke authentic responses and are a major aid to acculturation. We have also noted that their topicality is both an advantage and a disadvantage (which may be partially overcome) and that their inherent difficulty must be recognized.

Perhaps it would be appropriate at this stage to discuss the use of newspapers from a more methodologically conscious standpoint.

Newspapers and methodology

If there is one methodological point that almost everyone agrees on at present—Chomskyan innateness theorists, Krashen, the applied linguists, language teachers at the chalkface, and those we actually teach—it is that learning should be relatively natural.

Let's try to think about what 'natural' might mean in the classroom by considering a particular activity (4.10, 'Captions').

The teacher prepares for this activity by bringing as many different newspaper photographs of people in the news as there are learners in the class. In the lesson itelf, the teacher first lists on the board all the captions that accompanied the photographs and asks the students to copy them down and work out the meanings of any they do not understand among themselves and with the help of dictionaries. Then the learners each take a picture and circulate, suggesting possible captions for each others' pictures.

Having recently used this activity in a class that was being observed by a colleague from overseas, I was anxious to get his reaction. It surprised me: 'I think you should exploit the captions more,' he said. 'I'm sure not all the learners understood all of them. You could explain them tomorrow perhaps.'

Thinking about his comment afterwards, it occurred to me that perhaps he was drawing attention to the difference between the way he would work in his EFL classroom in a non-English-speaking country and the way I was working in my ESL-ish one in Britain. For him, authentic materials are a scarce resource to be 'exploited' to the full; and his learners expect everything to be 'explained' before the next topic is introduced. For me, the ESL context seems a more natural way to learn a language—by no means everything is fully understood, by no means everything that is there is used, just what is most relevant or appropriate. So that although the learners will usually be able to use dictionaries if they want to, they will never be expected to understand every word they read. In a comparable way, when I read a newspaper as a native speaker, I do not read every caption, nor do I try to work out its appropriacy and range of possible meanings: I am content to let most of what passes in front of me go by more or less unnoticed. This is why it makes sense to use newspapers as a stimulus for activities rather than as texts for comprehension and exploitation.

Most language teachers work in the EFL classroom, of course, and must sometimes feel that they have a harder task than the teacher in the ESL classroom, with all its sense of surrounding cultural richness and its stress on realistic, acculturated language behaviour. But whether, from a strictly sociolinguistic perspective, we work in an English as a Foreign Language context in a country such as China or in an English as a Second Language context in a country such as Kenya, newspapers certainly encourage us to work in this more 'natural' way. This is partly because they are plentiful enough even in EFL contexts for us to be able to use them relatively prodigally.

There seems also to be an interesting parallel with the teaching of literature. Do we see a foreign literature as essentially difficult, different, and exotic, in effect a long list of opaque vocabulary items and descriptions of semi-incomprehensible behaviour to be interpreted for us by a teacher who knows what a daffodil is and why Wordsworth liked wandering about on mountains—in other words, the traditional, exam-orientated approach? Or do we present a foreign literature in such a way as to allow learners to meet it on relatively equal terms, even experientially perhaps? In the case of Wordsworth's poem 'Daffodils', this might mean asking our students to associate images with words like 'crowd', 'dance', and 'wealth' before reading the poem, and then seeing how the words meant something different to Wordsworth. Of course, foreign literature (any literature) is 'difficult' and of course English-language newspapers are 'difficult': this book recommends meeting that difficulty not by 'exploiting' and 'explaining' the exotic or strange, but in a more natural way, by acquiring a gradual familiarity with it and by looking out for those things that students can relate to as people.

My overseas colleague's comment on the 'Captions' class also raises another very important issue: that the same newspaper materials can often be used in a very wide range of ways. This has two consequences:

1 One needs to think very carefully about the methodological implications of anything one does: for example, how differently will things work if (1) the two halves of your divided stories are blu-tacked to the wall to be re-united with each other by the learners, or (2) each learner has half a story and has to find the other half by circulating and asking fellow-students 'yes/no' questions?

2 The same text or picture can sometimes be used in a succession of activities, each of them depending on the level of understanding reached in the preceding one. Thus materials that initially seem too difficult can, if carefully approached, eventually be understood fully. When that happens, the resulting sense of achievement for the learner is very important and highly motivating.

So far I have argued for the importance of newspapers as a resource and for a relatively open or natural methodological stance. How then is this book organized?

How to use this book

The following chapters

The next chapter, 'Working creatively with newspapers', invites you to take stock of everything you already know about working with newspapers and suggests several ways of teaching yourself to be imaginative in the way you use newspaper materials. This is followed by five further chapters, each containing a wide range of ideas, activities, and exercises for the classroom. Some of these activities are centred on building confidence and familiarity, and some on text- and picture-based work. There is also a chapter dealing with projects based on newspaper materials, and finally a chapter with lots of person related ideas. Although not all the suggested activities will be new to every reader, you should find a good number of original, learner-centred ideas in these chapters: and you certainly will not find re-hashed versions of traditional ideas like writing to agony aunts and decoding small ads.

You may find one or two of the activities in Chapter 2, 'Building confidence and familiarity', particularly useful yourself if you are relatively unfamiliar with English-language newspapers and are not quite sure where to find what in them. Before starting work with your students, you may therefore like to try in particular 2.3, 'What's in a newspaper', which helps you to identify the various text types in a newspaper; 2.9, 'Where to put it', which gives practice in finding the exact location of a particular article type; and 2.30, 'Reading your own paper', which will help you to evaluate the differences between the mother-tongue newspapers you usually read and a typical English-language newspaper.

How each activity is organized

The organization of the activities in Chapters 2 to 6 of this book follows a common pattern. Information about each activity is given under up to nine headings:

Level

This indicates the minimum proficiency level at which the activity is likely to work. You can also use most of the activities in this book at any level above this minimum since the activities themselves are equally interesting to all levels of learner. Whenever this is the case, it is indicated by giving the minimum level, for example, 'Upper-elementary', followed by 'and above'.

Time

I have tried to give a reasonable *average* working time for each activity. This should enable you to skim through looking for activities that fit the time available to you. Of course, we all work at different speeds and expect slightly different things of our learners, and in many cases you may be able to speed up or slow down an activity to fit your needs.

Materials

This tells you what materials you will need for the activity. In the case of newspapers, it also tells you whether you need only cuttings, or complete newspapers, or even, occasionally, that day's newspapers.

Skills

This heading tells you which language skills (for example, 'discussion', 'reading') are promoted in the activity. It should help you to balance the time you allocate to each skill area over a course of several lessons.

Activity

This describes the newspaper-related skill which is practised in the activity. In a sense, this heading captures the purpose of the lesson. This may vary greatly from one activity to another. In one it may be to familiarize students with the layout of a newspaper, in another to recognize biased writing, in a third to understand the relationship between headline and story, for example.

Preparation

Any materials you need to get together (see Materials above) or anything you need to organize in the classroom before the lesson are described under this heading.

Procedure

Each activity is described step-by-step so that you can follow this plan in the classroom.

Variations

This indicates where you can vary the standard procedure to make the task a slightly different one. Where a lesson requires the use of a photocopier, this section may describe an equivalent activity that can be done without a photocopier.

Comments

Sometimes there are special circumstances under which a lesson works especially well, or a tip that is worth remembering, or some hidden purpose or unexpected outcome.

These headings are not used in Chapter 1 since this chapter is about taking stock of your existing knowledge and does not describe classroom activities in a step-by-step way. Instead, this chapter invites you to think about and summarize your existing knowledge.

The headings in Chapter 5, 'Project work', are sometimes slightly different, reflecting the ongoing nature of many of the activities in this Chapter.

When to use this book

When you use this book will depend to some extent on the context in which you work. Here are some possibilities, with the most cautious listed at the beginning and the most daring at the end. (You will probably want to try the cautious experiments first before going on to the more adventurous ones.)

- You could try one of the activities in Chapter 3, 'Working with texts', one day in place of the kind of text-based activity you would usually do.
- You could try one of the activities in Chapter 6, 'Personal responses', in place of a paired discussion activity.
- You could introduce newspapers into your syllabus gradually, in which case you should find useful ideas in Chapter 2, 'Building confidence and familiarity'.
- You could make your next project an ongoing newspaper-based one, in which case you should find useful ideas in Chapter 5, 'Project work'.
- If you want to do a special unit on newspapers over several weeks of a regular two-, three-, or four-lesson-a-week course, or if you are working on a two- or three-week intensive course in Britain and you want to spend a fair amount of time on newspapers, you should find useful ideas in Chapters 2, 3, 4, and 6.

Sequencing activities

There are a number of ways in which you could sequence the activities in this book:

- each separate chapter, for example, contains activities of a common type, so one could work on a set of activities from the same chapter;
- learners could practise a skill (scanning, matching, summarizing, predicting, etc.) by working on a sequence of activities with the same skill focus;
- you could choose a sequence of activities with a similar activity focus, or a sequence where the activity focus develops through a series of stages. These are all straightforward ways of putting together a suite of activities with a self-evident logical relationship to each other.

Another way you might like to try, which I have found particularly successful, is to select activities that enable the students to get in deeper stage by stage. For example, if you were working with the confidence-building activities in Chapter 2, you might progress from 2.7, 'Hide and seek', where the students work in pairs and follow instructions that lead them to stories chosen by their colleagues, to 2.12, 'Questions and advice', where pairs of students actually cut out a story and together write a suggestion directed at someone in it. This sequence could be extended with 6.11, 'Classifying stories', where each individual student cuts out a story and classifies it by colour, and then with 6.14, 'A story I relate to', where each student associates a flow of memories with an object and then connects one of these memories with one of the stories that classmates had chosen in the preceding activity.

This sequence progresses from pair to individual work and from reading stories to cutting them out. It also progresses from finding signposted stories, through commenting on stories, to associating them first with something relatively arbitrary (colours), and then with something much more personal (memories and experience). In this way, each activity acts as a springboard for the next one in the sequence. It is possible to make many such sequences of activities that reflect your own interests and enthusiasms and which take the learners progressively from outside to inside newspapers.

As you start to work with this book, you will probably find three things that surprise you at first :

Firstly, the point of each activity is simply to do it. All of the activities promote the confident use of newspaper materials so that if part of an activity consists of reading selected articles for ten minutes, this may be a sufficient activity in itself and will not always have an ulterior aim. You may have to get used to not asking yourself questions like, 'What does this lead to?' or 'What grammar points are being taught here?' or even, 'So what?' and instead accept that the students are listening, speaking, reading and writing in ways that are natural and authentic.

Secondly, newspaper extracts are only included when they are needed to illustrate a point, and I have not therefore supplied ready-made cuttings for you to work with. This means that you, or your students, have to supply the newspaper materials. There are several reasons for this: (1) students are much more motivated when they choose their own stories to work with, as most of the activities in this book require; (2) unless students become accustomed literally to getting their hands dirty on and finding their own way around newspapers, they will never learn to read an English-language newspaper for themselves; (3) this book will continue to be useful to you for much longer if the ideas are freed of particular texts, which in as little as two or three years will be out-of-date and inauthentic. At the end of Chapter 1, there are a number of suggestions to help you build up your own newspaper resource bank. These will be especially helpful if you are working in a non-English-speaking country.

Thirdly, you will rarely find that the different working speeds of individual students is a problem. This is because, apart from Chapter 6 which contains mostly individual activities, virtually all the activities in this book involve pair or small group work. This means that even when a group contains a slower reader, the others can be getting on with another part of the task. Where time-keeping is important, I have indicated how long to allow. This usually occurs in open-ended activities so that everyone will have done enough in the recommended time to be able to proceed to the next stage. And if you tell the students how long they have in advance, they usually finish early!

Finally, you will find detailed practical hints in the last part of Chapter 1, which should help you when working with the activities in this book.

For many teachers, this book will be seen as providing supplementary ideas which can be added to the regular teaching repertoire. These ideas have the merit of being stimulating, learner-centred, and at the same time materials-based.

1 Working creatively with newspapers

This short chapter is a bridge between the Introduction and the following chapters, which each contain about twenty classroom ideas under a specific chapter heading. Its purpose is to enable you to take stock of your existing knowledge and think about the kinds of new ideas that you could introduce into your classroom. From time to time, I will be asking you to stop reading and to make a short list of any ideas you have worked with in your own classroom. You will need a piece of paper and a pen.

Newspapers in coursebooks

Let's begin by thinking about the classroom ideas you may be familiar with from the newspaper related ideas found in coursebooks. For example, in *Blueprint* (Longman, 1990), Brian Abbs and Ingrid Freebairn frequently use both real and simulated newspaper materials to introduce units. Their theme usually serves as the key theme for the unit and they are typically read for comprehension before the unit moves on to various kinds of language practice work.

Stop and think for a couple of minutes about any newspaper-related ideas you have come across in the coursebooks you have used.

Look back over your list of ideas. Did they work well? What, if anything, did they lack?

Newspapers and English for Specific Purposes

Perhaps you have taught English for Specific Purposes and used a coursebook that contained newspaper materials. For example, in *Study Writing* (CUP, 1987) Liz Hamp-Lyons and Ben Heasley often use long newspaper extracts which the students read in a directed way to help them understand the structure or organization of the text. In this way they become more aware of the principles of structure and organization in their own writing.

Stop and think for a minute about other newspaper-based, ESP activities that you have come across.

Look back over your list: how relevant did you find these ideas? Did the students like working in this way? Why were these ideas more suited to ESP than to general language teaching? Were you already familiar with any of them?

Newspaper materials resource books

You may even be one of the small number of teachers who have worked with a newspaper materials resource book such as Janice Abbott's *Meet the Press* (CUP, 1981), which is unfortunately now out of print, or Barry Baddock's *Scoop* (Pergamon, 1984). Both these books contain a range of exercises and activities based on newspaper extracts that are supplied in the book. If you have worked with this sort of book, consider the following questions: Why did you choose this book? What proportion of your classwork was based on it? How well did it work? Did you supplement it with other newspaper materials? How imaginative did you find it?

If you have not worked with a newspaper-specific book of this kind before, here is a typical scanning exercise from *Meet the Press*:

---

1   Look at the article 'Chips are down for jobs' which follows. Before beginning to read the article, read question (a) carefully. Quickly scan the article for the answer. Underline the word, phrase, or sentence which answers the question. Repeat for all the questions. Do not worry about detail that is not directly related to the meaning to it in the context of the article.

     a)   What are silicon chips?
     b)   What kind of worries were fashionable before the silicon chip revolution?
     c)   Who discussed the problem of the effect of the microprocessor on employment, in Nice last week?
     d)   How many occupations could, in theory, be replaced by microprocessors?
     e)   What does Dr George Champine think will happen?
     f)   What does Carolyn Hayman think will happen?
     g)   What trivial thing can microprocessors already do?
     h)   What will happen to the British economy if it does not accept and use microprocessors?

2   Divide into groups with three or four people in each and discuss the following questions. Be prepared to report back to the whole class giving reasons for your opinions and conclusions.

     a)   In which fields and for what purposes are microprocessors already being used?
     b)   In which fields and for what purposes do you think they will be used in the future?
     c)   In what ways could microprocessors change our everyday life?
     d)   It has been said that the transistor was the first revolution in electronics, and the microprocessor is the second. Do you agree with this statement? Why? Why not?

Chips are down for jobs

from NIGEL HAWKES, our Science Correspondent in Nice

ARE FIVE million jobs in Britain about to be replaced by tiny chips of silicon? It is a prospect that is sending shivers down the spines of Ministers, civil servants, academics and trade union leaders.

The silicon chips are, of course, microprocessors, minute but highly sophisticated electronic circuits suited to an almost infinite variety of applications, from the humble pocket calculator to the control of entire automated factories and warehouses.

The effects the microprocessor will have on employment are the subject of intense argument. For those who like to keep their worries in fashion, the silicon chip revolution has taken over from pollution, the energy crisis, and the bomb as a subject of concern.

For three days last week a small group which included Government, political, trade union, industry and press representatives discussed the problem at the Sperry Univac Executive Centre at Saint-Paul-de-Vence, near Nice.

Almost everybody agreed there was a problem. The list of jobs that could in theory be replaced by microprocessors is long and alarming.

A report prepared for the Computer, Systems and Electronics Requirements Board, but still unpublished, lists 29 occupations at risk, starting with proof readers and including postmen, draughtsmen, secretaries, filing clerks, meter readers, plate-printers, assembly workers, warehousemen, sales clerks and many others.

But the real issue is not whether jobs will be lost in some sectors of the economy—that is a normal effect of advancing technology—but whether they will be replaced by other jobs in the new industries the microprocessor will replace. There the arguments begin.

The American and Japanese view is that concern over the issue has been exaggerated. Dr George Champine, director of Advanced Systems for Sperry Univac in the United States, claimed that 'literally thousands' of new products would emerge from the microprocessor revolution.

'Every time technology advances people forecast unemployment. The mechanical reaper, the cotton gin, and the first computers 30 years ago were all supposed to cause massive unemployment,' Dr Champine said, 'But it didn't happen.'

Miss Carolyn Hayman, a young economist from the Central Policy Review Staff—the Government's 'Think Tank'—also took a relatively optimistic view. She thought it likely that the service industries could continue to absorb people displaced.

The gloomy viewpoint was put by Dr Ray Curnow, of the First Policy Research Unit at Sussex University, who said that Britain needs to find new jobs at a staggering rate, equal to 6 per cent a year, just to stay where it is.

'It will be economic to use the microprocessor to do the most trivial things,' he said.

One of the trivial things microprocessors can already do is to dispense cocktails. At the press of a button the 'electronic bartender' will deliver a perfect Bloody Mary or a Martini mixed to individual taste. Participants at the seminar were stirred rather than shaken by this news.

The Japanese Government has switched its emphasis away from heavy industries like shipbuilding and steel making and towards microprocessor-based products.

So the option of going slowly in Britain seems to be closed, unless we retreat into a siege economy and ban imports. Either we embrace the microprocessor and lose jobs through displacement or we reject it and lose jobs through a catastrophic loss of international competitiveness. It is a challenging and alarming choice.

from *The Observer*   *chips are down*: the time has come to face the problem

How well do you think this exercise would work with your students?

Many teachers would perhaps 'top and tail' an exercise like this with their own ideas. For example, you could begin by explaining that the class was going to read a newspaper article whose title was five words long. You could give the students the first word, 'Chips', and ask them to guess the other four (although in this case, this might be a very difficult exercise!). Once the title was guessed, you could ask your students to tell you what they expected the story to be about. You might justify adapting the given materials on the grounds that the activity is a kind of pre-reading task which prepares the students for the article they are going to study. And it is authentic in the sense that in the real world we see and think a little bit about the headline before we decide how (and even whether) to read the story.

Having completed Janice Abbott's scanning and discussion exercises, you could make the activity more person-related by asking your students to think about their own contact with and use of microprocessors. This might be justified on the grounds that it helps the students to relate a foreign language newspaper article to their own lives. It is also an authentic activity in the sense that we would think of our own use of microprocessors if we had read this article.

Stop a minute and evaluate the 'topping and tailing' activities suggested above. Are they good ideas? How are they different from Janice Abbott's ideas? Is this the sort of way you tend to work with given materials?

When you have thought about these three questions, take another couple of minutes and make a list of all the ways you have adapted or added to the newspaper-based materials you have come across in coursebooks, ESP books or (even) newspaper resource books.

The focus of *Meet the Press* is reading. In particular, the author lists skimming, scanning, reading for central ideas, and guessing the meaning of words as the four principal skills practised in the book. What other skills do you think could be practised when working with newspaper materials? What kind of activity would give practice in each skill?

In *Scoop*, the author lists both specifically newspaper-based activities and general activities which can be done with newspaper materials. His lists include:

Newspaper-specific	**General discussion**
Compiling a front page	Vocabulary development
Making headlines	Practising syntax
Learning abbreviations	Comparing and contrasting
Writing problem letters	Comprehension
Writing captions	Summarizing
Simplified punctuation	Analysing
Understanding ads	Role play
Preparing a weather forecast	

You may well have tried some of these when using newspapers, and have other ideas of your own to add.

Working with newspapers

Most teachers are occasional users of newspaper materials. Here is a list of some of the better known activities that have not already been mentioned:

- writing and replying to small ads;
- writing and replying to letters to agony aunts;
- re-ordering jumbled paragraphs;
- re-ordering jumbled cartoon strips;
- completing cartoon speech bubbles;
- predicting horoscopes for class members;
- matching property ads with students' needs;
- replying to job ads;
- devising appropriate penalties for criminals.

These may well include ideas you added to the last list. Now that your memory has been jogged, can you add three or four more ideas?

Working with newspaper stories

Perhaps you have taken a particular newspaper story and worked with it in a number of ways. Let's take the story 'Chauvinist husband divorced' as an example:

'Chauvinist' husband divorced

The "male chauvinism" of Mr Andrew Hulford earnt his wife Jacqueline a divorce yesterday.

Mrs Hulford liked to go out and meet people and have some independence. Mr Hulford, aged 44, believed a wife's place was in the home and her duty was to look after husband and children.

When Mrs Hulford, aged 33, dressed up to go out, her husband made "snide" comments about smartening herself up to try to attract other men.

If she met other men, he would become jealous, Mr Justice Sheldon said in the High Court Family Division. He "begrudged her any independent life".

The judge said that Mr Hulford had behaved "reprehensibly". His wife could no longer be expected to put up with "the plague of repetitive suspicion".

Although Mr Hulford denied behaving badly and that his marriage had broken down. Mr Justice Sheldon granted Mrs Hulford a decree nisi.

The couple, who have a young son and daughter and live in the same house at Elsenham, Essex, married in 1977. Both had been married before.

Mr Justice Sheldon said that about three years ago there was a "serious rift in their relationship". They stopped making love in 1982.

Mr Hulford said afterwards: "I don't see myself as having the attitudes of a Victorian husband.

"I do not accept that I was domineering or chauvinist. I just consider myself to be an ordinary English husband. I like to come home from work and see my wife and kids there. And I like my wife to stay at home with me in the evening. Any husband would.

"I still think there is hope for our marriage even after what has happened. I still love her."

How is this story different from the feature article from *Meet the Press*? How could you use it? Stop and think for a couple of minutes, and then make a list of all the activities you can think of.

Look back at your list and check to see if you had any of the following ideas:

- staging an interview with Andrew and Jacqueline, separately or together;
- recording audio (or, if possible, video) statements by Andrew and Jacqueline explaining the problem—this could be used as a pre-reading 'text';
- rewriting the story in the style of a popular paper;
- rewriting the story from a partisan perspective—perhaps under headlines like 'My husband was a Male Chauvinist Pig' or, 'My wife was a tart';
- working on the vocabulary, directly or indirectly—by asking the students to supply examples of 'snide comments' and 'reprehensible behaviour';
- working on the culture—for example, by asking the students to draw or describe 'an ordinary English husband', or Mr. Justice Sheldon, and comparing this with their own culture;
- writing the questions they would like to ask each of them;
- writing the questions they would like to ask the judge, the couple's children, their previous spouses;
- staging (and video-ing) a discussion/role-play on divorce, and this case in particular, involving parties such as a marriage counsellor, a priest, a judge;
- discussing the issue of an 'independent life' in marriage;
- drawing up a sample 'Marriage contract' to be signed by couples contemplating marriage;
- advising Andrew and Jacqueline as they each contemplate a third marriage;
- speculating about the nature of the 'serious rift';
- apportioning blame and taking sides.

What we have just been thinking about is essentially an exploitative use of a newspaper article. Now find your own article, read it carefully, and then make a list of exploitative uses to which it might be put.

Imaginative newspaper work

By the time you have got this far into the chapter you should have a long list of what might be called 'conventional' uses of newspaper materials. The rest of this book is not about these conventional ideas: it is more about how newspapers may be used naturally as one of a number of sources of authentic language in a communicative classroom. It is not so much understanding texts that will be important, but the stimulation they provide for learners to think, talk, and write about the things that matter to them. Perhaps you have used newspapers in these more imaginative ways in your own classroom. Take a couple of minutes to think about this and then make two lists, one of any imaginative ideas you have tried yourself, the other of any you have heard about from colleagues but have not actually tried in your own classroom.

By this stage, you should have listed virtually every newspaper idea you have ever used or heard of. (I hope you have not also listed too many of those that you will find in the following chapters!)

Thinking creatively

The Introduction drew attention to the importance of developing a repertoire of activities and of becoming good at creative planning. Very often teacher development sessions or training days provide ideal opportunities to develop these skills together with colleagues. Here are three helpful brainstorming ideas suitable for a small group of language teachers:

1 Cut out a newspaper story or feature article for each teacher in your group. Sit in a circle. Each teacher starts with one of the cuttings and a blank 'Ideas' sheet and writes one idea for using the cutting on the sheet. Each teacher then passes the cutting and sheet one place round the circle. Continue with the same cuttings until the ideas stop flowing. At that stage, each person reads out the ideas on the sheet in front of them while their colleagues copy down on their sheets any that would be suitable for the cutting they have.

2 Make up a series of sheets of paper headed:

Things to do with news stories
Things to do with letters pages
Things to do with feature articles
Things to do with cartoons
Things to do with pictures
Things to do with advertisements

You will need one differently headed sheet for each teacher in your group plus three or four more. Distribute the sheets around a large table, take away the chairs, and ask your colleagues to brainstorm ideas on each sheet. For some reason this works much better if each person moves round the table when the urge takes them and leaves the sheets in their original positions rather than if everyone sits and passes the sheets round a circle.

3 Using single keywords or short phrases, draw up a list of general classroom activities that minimize the role of the teacher. Try to make your own list first before adding in any items from the list below that you may not have thought of.

matching pictures and language	jigsaw reading/listening
games	survey work
reducing long messages to telegrams	video work
picture dictation	questionnaires
starters	problem solving
counselling	horoscopes
reconstructing telegrams	simulation
stories from sounds	storytelling
stories from objects	communication through image
interviews	discussion
melodrama	

In your group, work through the list item by item discussing all the possible ways (if any) in which the activity could be applied to newspapers.

If you try these three ideas, they should add considerably to the list of activities you were already familiar with.

Material requirements and conditions for creative work

The rest of this chapter makes a number of points about imaginative ways of working with newspapers.

Let's begin with a concrete idea. In Chapter 6, you will find an exercise called 'Classifying stories' (6.11). Essentially, each student is required to find a story they are interested in, decide whether it is a 'blue', 'green', or 'red' story, glue it on a sheet of paper, and explain why it has been classified under the chosen colour. The stories are then displayed on the classroom walls for general reading.

Although the idea sounds very simple, there are a number of important conditions that must be met if it is to work:

– you must have an abundant supply of newspapers;
– you must be prepared for the newspapers to be cut up;
– you must have the means of gluing them to sheets of paper and then displaying them on the walls;

- you must work in an institution where students are allowed to move around the classroom freely.

These conditions are essentially to do with materials and resources.

More subtle are a second set of conditions that are to do with your beliefs about learning:

- you must accept that each student will be working on a different story;
- you must accept that each student will have a different criterion for choosing and then classifying a story;
- you must accept that making what appears to be a relatively arbitrary connection between a colour and a story requires the students to think hard about what they are reading;
- you must accept that there is no quantifiable language of the type specified in a syllabus which you can say anyone has formally learned in this lesson;
- you must accept that you are playing a facilitative role only and that what the students learn will not result from your formal teaching;
- your ultimate aim must be to get students to buy and read English-language newspapers for themselves rather than to use a newspaper extract for a carefully devised language practice exercise;
- you need to recognize that some students are not used to this way of working and may not in the early stages accept that it works effectively;
- you must accept that a large slice of class time will be spent on silent reading.

The same sort of points could be made about most of the exercises in this book. If you read one them and imagine how it would work in your classroom, and you find yourself saying when you have read it, 'So what?', remember that the purpose of this book is to provide exercises that will turn language learners into autonomous readers of English-language newspapers. Each exercise is therefore justified as it stands —you do not have to worry about whether it practises some language point or specific skill.

Specific material resources

Working creatively with newspapers often assumes that you have access to specific material resources. These include:

1 A **supply of newspapers**—usually it does not matter at all if they are old newspapers. Remember that English-language newspapers are published in virtually every country in the world as well as widely exported from English-speaking countries. The Appendix contains a list of some of the better known English-language newspapers available in countries where English is not a

national language. Since there is virtually certain to be at least one cheap English-language newspaper wherever in the world you are working, why not ask each student to bring one into class with them?

2 A **'Story Bank'** of several dozen, even several hundred, newspaper stories and articles. These are best mounted on sheets of paper or card. You can build up your Story Bank by collecting stories from the cannibalised newspapers that are left over after many of the exercises in this book. Often an exercise asks a student to select a story that interests them from a newspaper—the activity just described, 'Classifying stories' (6.11), is a typical example of this sort of exercise. At the end of the class, you can put all the stories into your Story Bank. You will probably be surprised at how rapidly you build up a Story Bank as a by-product of actually doing the activities in class.

3 A somewhat smaller **'Picture Bank'**, including pictures from colour magazines as well as black and white newspaper ones. You may well have such a resource already. If you have not, this is a good time to start, as a Picture Bank comes in useful for many other classroom activities.

4 Access to a **photocopier** is useful, although most activities have a Variation where no photocopier is required.

5 A **supply of paper** to glue stories to—it does not have to be new paper as long as it is clean on one side.

6 **Glue** for sticking stories to paper.

7 A means of displaying stories and student work on classroom walls, such as blu-tack or, for display boards, drawing pins. If you are not able to stick things to the walls, you can usually display them on desks instead.

To sum up: if you want to work creatively with newspapers and if your ultimate aim is to get your students to read newspapers for themselves, you will need a sufficient supply of:

- **newspapers**, for students to select their own stories from;
- **imaginative ideas**, which the following chapters should provide and to which you can add once you see how easy thinking them up can be;
- the **confidence** to allow the students to teach themselves.

2 Building confidence and familiarity

The twenty-eight activities in this chapter share a common purpose. They are all designed to make your students feel that they can handle newspapers.

I have not tried to arrange them according to whether they build confidence or establish familiarity since the two notions really go hand in hand, although you will find a few activities that are designed principally to build confidence, such as 2. 1, 'When I hit the headlines', and a few whose main aim is to establish familiarity, such as 2.4, 'New names'.

There is a certain logic to the order in which they are presented, however. The first two activities draw on your students' past contributions to newspapers. Activities 2.3–2.6 help the students to gain familiarity with the contents of English-language newspapers, while activities 2.7–2.9 focus on the location of the different types of text in a newspaper. The largest group of activities, 2.10–2.18, focuses on ways of reacting to the content of particular texts. Activities 2.19 and 2.20 relate texts to para-texts such as headlines and posters. Although quite different in character, activities 2.21–2.25 are all follow-up activities, while the final set of five activities focuses on evaluation and deciding what one wants to read. I recommend the Comments at the end of the last activity in the chapter, 'Reading your own paper' (2.30), which stress the usefulness and importance of getting the students to buy their own newspapers.

You will find that many of the activities in this chapter involve letting the students choose the articles they want to work with. This also implies that they are at the same time rejecting all those they do not choose. As they work though a newspaper rejecting and selecting, they are already establishing a working familiarity with the materials which should support and enable the activities in the chapter.

2.1 When I hit the headlines

LEVEL	**Lower-intermediate and above**
TIME	**25 minutes**
MATERIALS	**None**
SKILLS	**Exchanging information in pairs**
ACTIVITY	**Relating newspapers to personal experience**

PROCEDURE

1 Each student makes a list of every occasion they were in the newspapers: this could include stories involving themselves, photographs, any letters they have had published, advertisements they placed, etc.

2 The students then circulate freely, exchanging their newspaper experiences with those of classmates.

VARIATION

For business English students a possible variation is to list all the occasions their company has been in the newspapers.

COMMENTS

This is a good icebreaker: by building a bridge between learners' knowledge of mother-tongue newspapers and the English-language newspaper work that is to follow, it helps to dispel the students' sense that English-language newspapers are another world.

2.2 The letter I never wrote (until now)

LEVEL	**Upper-intermediate and above**
TIME	**30 minutes**
MATERIALS	**None**
SKILLS	**Letter writing**
ACTIVITY	**Learning how a reader can contribute to a newspaper**

PROCEDURE

1 Ask the students to spend two to three minutes recalling a time when they really felt like writing a letter to a newspaper but did not actually write it.

2 Ask the students to work in groups of three to five. Make sure that at least one student in each group can remember a time when they wanted to write to a newspaper.

3 The students who wanted to write a letter explain to the other members of their group what they wanted to write about, and the group decides which of the letters to write collectively.

4 When the letters have been written, they can be read aloud and then displayed on the wall.

COMMENTS

Even if the students were not brave enough or had no time actually to write the letter, they have now done it—and in English too. This fosters a sense of achievement.

2.3 What's in a newspaper

LEVEL

Intermediate and above

TIME

30–40 minutes

MATERIALS

One newspaper for every five students

SKILLS

Making lists, skim reading

ACTIVITY

Identifying newspaper text types

PROCEDURE

1 Ask the students to work in groups of four to five. Each group makes a list of all the types of article one expects to find in a newspaper. Because the students are likely to have problems with the English names for some of these categories, it may help to encourage them to think of the names in their mother tongue first (you may then have to translate for them). After five to ten minutes, check that each group has the essential categories, including home and foreign news stories, feature articles (medical, social, domestic, personal, cultural, and artistic), leaders and comment columns, announcements of births, marriages, and deaths, obituaries, readers' letters, business news, advertisements, TV and radio reviews and programme schedules, weather reports, crosswords and other readers' competitions, cartoons, sports pages, review articles, law reports.

2 Hand out a newspaper to each group and ask them to spend 10 minutes finding an example of each type of article.

3 Ask each group to spend a further 10 minutes looking for any features that do not fit their original list of categories. They should add these categories to their list.

COMMENTS

This is an important familiarization activity which helps the students to classify and put a name to each type of article in a newspaper.

2.4 New names

LEVEL	**Upper-elementary and above**
TIME	**30–40 minutes**
MATERIALS	**One newspaper per student**
SKILLS	**Scanning, listing and abstracting, summarizing**
ACTIVITY	**Acquiring knowledge about those in the news**

PROCEDURE

1 Give each student a different news page and ask them to skim through, ringing the names of every person mentioned.

2 Ask each student to make a list of all the names they have ringed that they were already familiar with.

3 Ask each student to make a second list of the names of all the people they had not heard of before. After each name they should add a one-line description of the person, based on what they can find out by reading the news story.

COMMENTS

This activity promotes confidence in two ways: first, it demonstrates to the students how much they already know, and then it encourages them to find out how easy it is to discover new information.

2.5 Names in the news

LEVEL	**Intermediate and above**
TIME	**40–45 minutes**
MATERIALS	**One newspaper for every four students**
SKILLS	**Abstracting, summarizing , and classifying**
ACTIVITY	**Acquiring familiarity with people in the news**

PROCEDURE

1 Ask the students to work in groups of four and give a newspaper to each group. Ask the groups to find the names of as many people as they can, and write down each name, together with a one-line biography, on a separate small piece of paper. For example:

George Bush, President of the USA
Sally Smith, a nurse who works in Saudi Arabia
Madonna, a rock singer and film star.

Allow this to continue until each group has at least twenty names.

2 Ask each group to classify their names under one of the following four categories: 'Politician', 'Sports player', 'Entertainer', 'Ordinary person'.

3 Ask the groups to form a large circle. Make sure that each group stays together in the circle. One group lays down one of their names in the centre of the circle and reads the one-line biography aloud.

4 The next group must then 'follow suit' by placing another name in the same category on top of the first name and reading the name and biography aloud. Alternatively, the next group may 'change suit' by contributing a person whose first name or surname begins with the same letter as the first name or surname of the previous person. For example, one sequence could go:

George Bush, politician, President of the USA
Mikhail Gorbachev, politician, former President of the Soviet Union
(Both 'Bush' and 'Gorbachev' are politicians.)

Paul Gascoigne, sports player, an English footballer.
(Both 'Gorbachev' and 'Gascoigne' begin with 'G'.)

If a group cannot contribute a name, they miss a turn.

5 Continue until no group can contribute a name or until one group 'wins' by laying down all its names.

COMMENTS

Unless one knows who the newspapers are writing about, there is not a lot of point in reading them. This activity helps the students to become familiar with the people English-language newspapers write about. You can follow up this activity in the next lesson by asking the students to find further mentions of the people identified in this activity.

2.6 Understanding what we don't understand

LEVEL

Intermediate and above

TIME

40 minutes

MATERIALS

One newspaper, access to a photocopier

SKILLS

Resolving difficulties in texts

ACTIVITY

Discovering that even difficult newspaper materials are not an insuperable challenge

PREPARATION

Make enough copies of a news page for each student in the class. (You may have to copy the page on to two sheets of paper.)

PROCEDURE

1 Give each student a photocopy and ask them to underline anything they do not understand.

2 Ask the students to work in pairs and try to help each other with their difficulties.

3 Encourage pairs to combine into groups of four to try to resolve any outstanding difficulties.

4 Finally, make time for a whole class discussion of any unresolved problems.

VARIATION

If you do not have access to a photocopier, you can give a different news page to each group of four to five students, who then work together on trying to identify and resolve any difficulties they encounter.

COMMENTS

This activity promotes a self-help attitude and ensures that you contribute only at the end of the process when the students have discovered what they really do need help with.

2.7 Hide and seek

LEVEL

Intermediate and above

TIME

30–60 minutes

MATERIALS

One newspaper for every two students, address labels (optional)

SKILLS

Reading and summarizing

ACTIVITY

Finding one's way around a newspaper

PROCEDURE

1 Ask the students to work in pairs. Give each pair a newspaper. Ask them to find a story or feature which they think would interest other members of the class.

2 Each pair should write a one- or two-sentence instruction indicating roughly where the story can be found in the newspaper and mentioning some fact from the story. For example:

> This is a story from the sports pages. A record gets broken.

> This is a love story involving a grandmother. It can be found in the middle pages of the newspaper.

If you have address labels or 'post-it' stickers, these instructions can be written on a label which is then stuck to the top left-hand corner of the front page of the newspaper.

3 Pairs exchange their newspapers and instructions and the receiving pairs now seek the hidden story. This stage can be repeated as often as you like.

VARIATION 1

Instead of Stage 3, ask the students to place their newspapers in a pile in the middle of the classroom and allow them 10–15 minutes to find and read as many of the stories as possible in the time. The race-against-time element adds a lot of fun to the activity.

VARIATION 2

Ask each pair to copy a sentence from their chosen story at Stage 2 instead of writing an instruction. This leads to a more time-consuming and slightly different kind of scanning activity at Stage 3.

2.8 Where to find it

LEVEL

Intermediate and above

TIME

15 minutes per item

MATERIALS

One newspaper for every three students

SKILLS

Skim reading and summarizing

ACTIVITY

Acquiring familiarity with the layout of individual pages and whole newspapers

PREPARATION

Take a newspaper and select one interesting article or story. Do not cut it out. Instead, write instructions on a piece of paper or card for each story explaining exactly where and in which newspaper it can be found. For example:

```
You will find this article on the Women's page
of the Guardian of 27th May 1991, in the second
column of the block headed 'Returning to work',
just below the feature about company car
drivers' habits.
```

Pin these instructions to the appropriate newspaper. Keep repeating this process, each time with a different newspaper, until you have found one story or article for every three students in the class.

PROCEDURE

1 Group the students in threes and give each group a newspaper with the instructions pinned to it.

2 Tell the groups to find their story or article, read it, and write a one-sentence summary of it.

3 This stage can be repeated as often as you like. Each group passes their newspaper and instructions to the next group. Later you can display the stories and summary sentences on the wall.

VARIATION

When the students have done this activity a few times, ask one group to choose the article and write the instructions for another group.

COMMENTS

This familiarization activity helps students to find their way around English-language newspapers.

Acknowledgement
This activity is based on one of John Morgan's ideas.

2.9 Where to put it

LEVEL

Upper-intermediate and above

TIME

30–40 minutes

MATERIALS

Two different days' copies of a newspaper for every five to six students

SKILLS

Reading, discussing, matching text and context

ACTIVITY

Locating different article types

PREPARATION

Cut out five different types of article (news story, feature, letter, sports report, etc.) from *one* copy of each of your titles. For each group of students in your class you will need one complete newspaper and five cut-out articles taken from a different day's copy of the same newspaper.

PROCEDURE

1 Ask the students to work in groups of five to six. Give each group one complete newspaper and the five articles cut out of the other copy of it.

2 Each group decides precisely where each article should be located in the copy of the newspaper they have in front of them. It may help the students to understand what they have to do if you tell them that each group should think like an editor and try to decide whereabouts in the paper each of the stories should be inserted (for example, 'Under foreign news, halfway down page 3 in the centre').

COMMENTS	If you have access to a number of different newspaper titles, you can give each group a different newspaper to work with. Otherwise, you can use the same title for all the groups.

2.10 Front pages

LEVEL	**Business English, intermediate and above**
TIME	**30–40 minutes**
MATERIALS	**Front pages of quality newspapers**
SKILLS	**Scanning and then intensive reading**
ACTIVITY	**Understanding personal implications of the news**
PROCEDURE	Ask the students to work in groups of four to five. Give each group two or three front pages. Ask the students to study them and make a detailed list of all the possible ways the news items might affect their work. This works particularly well if you ask the students to list short-, medium-, and long-term effects.
VARIATION	For general English classes, ask the students to trace out any possible implications for their own personal or working lives.

2.11 Reading for leisure/reading for work

LEVEL	**Business English, intermediate and above**
TIME	**40–50 minutes**
MATERIALS	**Two newspapers for every seven to eight students; glue**
SKILLS	**Task reading**
ACTIVITY	**Reading for real-life relevant information**
PROCEDURE	1 Make newspapers available. Ask each student to take part of a newspaper and look for a story which has implications for how they spend their leisure and a story which has implications for their work. The students will need to keep swapping their pages until they have all found their two stories, which should be cut out and glued to a single (large) sheet of paper.

2 Ask each student to spend a minute or two working out a connection between their two stories. This connection should be written down on the sheet to which the stories are glued.

3 Display the sheets on the wall and allow reading and discussion time.

2.12 Questions and advice

LEVEL

Intermediate and above

TIME

30–40 minutes

MATERIALS

One newspaper for every five students or your Story Bank (see page 28)

SKILLS

Careful reading, writing relevant questions and comments

ACTIVITY

Relating to people in newspaper stories

PROCEDURE

1 Give out newspapers or make your Story Bank available. Ask each student to cut out or select a story that interests them. They should write a question or a suggestion/piece of advice directed at one of the people in the story on a separate piece of paper.

2 The students leave their stories and questions or suggestions on their desks and circulate reading each other's stories. Each time they read a story, they add either a new question or a new suggestion/piece of advice.

VARIATION

The following make good homework tasks:
Day 1 Give each student eight to ten pages of newspaper to take home. They should write a question/piece of advice directed at one person on each page.

Day 2 The students exchange their homework and try to answer or respond to the questions/advice as though they were the people in the stories.

COMMENTS

If you provide the students with a selection of 'quality' and 'popular' newspapers and repeat this activity for a second time, you will almost certainly find a rush for the popular papers. Indeed, the more familiar your students become with a range of English-language newspapers, the more likely they are to prefer working with popular papers. This can be instructive for those of us who were accustomed as learners to being offered only extracts from quality newspapers. You will also find that this comment applies more strongly to the next activity.

2.13 Things I want to know

LEVEL	Intermediate and above
TIME	30+ minutes
MATERIALS	Several newspapers or your Story Bank (see page 28), glue
SKILLS	Reading, writing supplementary questions
ACTIVITY	Discovering what is included in, and omitted from, newspaper stories

PROCEDURE

1 Give out newspapers or make your Story Bank available. Ask each student to cut out a human interest story, glue it to a sheet of paper, and display it on the wall.

2 The students circulate, reading the stories and writing up questions designed to elicit interesting information not in the text.

EXAMPLE

Imagine a student had displayed the following story:

£35,000 FOR BOY OF SIX LABELLED A BRAT

Handicap kid's libel triumph

A BOY of six branded the "worst brat in Britain" by a newspaper won £35,000 libel damages yesterday.

Handicapped Jonathan Hunt was said to have been a "terror tot" who wrecked his parent's home, cut off his own ear and killed the family cat.

But the claims were lies. Tragic Jonathan — the youngest person in Britain ever to sue for libel — had behavioural problems after developing meningitis at birth.

Yesterday Jonathan's 36-year-old mother Josephine, said the stress of the case had helped cause the break-up of her marriage.

And the mother of four revealed that despite the payout she still could not afford treatment her son needs in the US.

The claims were made in the Sun newspaper, which was ordered by the High Court to pay costs.

An article called Jonathan Britain's "naughtiest kid" and quoted Josephine, of Sawsdon, Cambs, as saying: "He's a horror.

"My three others are perfectly normal. I keep asking myself, 'Why me?'"

Later, The Sun carried a letter from Josephine saying her son was handicapped, that he severed his ear in an accident and that the cat had died from sickness.

It was headlined "Monday moan."

Mrs Hunt, who shares the damages, wanted the award paid in a week. But The Sun asked for three weeks to pay because the cheque had to come from their Peterborough accounts HQ.

Mr Justice Otton ordered that the money should be paid as quickly as possible and said: "The Romans managed to get to Peterborough.

"I cannot accept that it will take this company 21 days to pay this cheque."

The kinds of questions fellow students write up might include:

> What other things did Jonathan do?
>
> Why did his naughtiness cause his parents' marriage to break up?
>
> How did the cat get ill?
>
> What was the accident that caused his ear to be cut off?
>
> Does Mrs Hunt plan to have any more children?

VARIATION

A possible follow-up activity is to take the stories and questions and rewrite the stories so as to include supposed answers to the questions.

Acknowledgement
This is one of John Morgan's ideas.

2.14 Probing human interest stories

LEVEL

Upper-intermediate and above

TIME

40–50 minutes

MATERIALS

Two human interest stories, access to a photocopier

SKILLS

Purposeful interactive writing

ACTIVITY

Understanding why people find themselves in the newspapers

PREPARATION

Choose two human interest stories involving people whose behaviour seems strange or unexpected. Make one copy of each for every two students in the class.

PROCEDURE

1 Ask the students to sit in a circle. Hand out each of the two stories alternately round the circle.

2 Each student reads their story, takes a sheet of paper, and writes a question on it addressed directly to one of the people in the story. The students should indicate who their questions are addressed to.

3 The stories and questions are now passed one place to the left, round the circle. Each student then writes a reply to the question in front of them in the role of the person in the story.

4 The stories, questions, and replies should be passed back to the student who wrote the question.

5 When the students receive the replies to their questions, they write comments or further questions and pass them back to their neighbour on the left for a response. Thus each student communicates in writing with both of their neighbours. Allow this to continue for up to 30 minutes.

6 Ask two or three pairs to read aloud or act out their 'written dialogues'.

VARIATION

If you do not have access to a photocopier, this activity is still possible. As long as each student gets a human interest story at Stage 1, the rest of the Procedure works fine. There are two advantages to working with photocopied stories though:

- it is less work for you to find two stories than to find enough for the whole class
- Stage 6 only works when everyone in the class knows the two stories.

COMMENTS

This activity enables the students to get inside the characters in a human interest story and try to understand their motives.

2.15 Which story next?

LEVEL

Intermediate and above

TIME

At least 30 minutes

MATERIALS

One newspaper for every five students, or your Story Bank (see page 28)

SKILLS

Accurate listening, spoken presentation

ACTIVITY

Connecting newspaper stories

PROCEDURE

1 Give out newspapers or make your Story Bank available. Ask each student to find a story that interests them and to spend two or three minutes making sure they can explain what it is about to fellow students.

2 Ask someone to explain what their story is about to the class. Tell the class that after the story has been explained, anyone with a similar story should explain theirs and that this process will continue without you intervening for 20 minutes or until all the stories have been explained, whichever occurs first.

COMMENTS

There are two important features of this activity: it gives the students confidence when they find they can interpret a newspaper story for their colleagues, and it makes them listen to each explanation carefully as they must judge whether their story relates to it. The continuous discourse is also pleasant to listen to as it has a developing theme and a variety of speakers. The whole amounts to more than the sum of the parts.

2.16 Categorizing stories

LEVEL

Intermediate and above

TIME

40 minutes

MATERIALS

One newspaper for every five students or your Story Bank (see page 28), glue

SKILLS

Reading, classifying, and justifying decisions

ACTIVITY

Responding to newspaper stories on an emotional level

PROCEDURE

1 Pair the students and give out newspapers or make your Story Bank available. Ask each pair to cut out a story that interests them. Each story should be glued to a sheet of paper.

2 Choose a category noun such as 'bird' and ask each pair to read their story carefully and decide which sort of bird characterizes it best. (For example, it might be a 'robin', a 'nightingale', an 'eagle', a 'magpie', a 'vulture', etc.) When they have decided, they should write the name of the bird and the reason for their decision on the back of the story.

3 Allow the students to keep taking stories and categorizing them for 30 minutes. This works well if you allow pairs to choose stories that other pairs have already read and categorized.

COMMENTS

1 Other category nouns that work well include 'sports', 'cars', 'furniture', 'clothes', and 'fruit'.

2 This activity looks forward to the person-related activities you will find in Chapter 6, 'Personal responses'.

2.17 Picture into story

LEVEL

Elementary and above

TIME

25 minutes

MATERIALS

One newspaper for every five students

SKILLS	**Reading, deciding on the most salient aspects of a text, matching picture and story**
ACTIVITY	**Matching picture and story**
PROCEDURE	1 Give out newspapers and ask each student to cut out a story that interests them.
	2 When everyone has done this, ask the students to draw a picture to represent their story.
	3 When the students have drawn their pictures, they display them on the wall and give you the stories.
	4 Redistribute the stories so that each student gets a new one. Ask them to find and remove the matching picture from the wall.
COMMENTS	If you do not have whole newspapers available, you can use old left-over newspaper pages or your Story Bank.

2.18 Culture and newspapers

LEVEL	**Intermediate and above**
TIME	**25–30 minutes**
MATERIALS	**One newspaper for every two students or your Story Bank (see page 28)**
SKILLS	**Reading for a purpose**
ACTIVITY	**Studying the relationship of culture and language in newspapers**
PROCEDURE	1 Pair the students and give one newspaper to each pair or make your Story Bank available. Ask each pair to find a story that they feel reflects the culture of an English-speaking society. Each pair cuts their story out, glues it to a sheet of paper, and explains on the sheet why the story reflects the society.
	2 The stories and explanations are displayed on the wall. Allow 10 minutes' reading time.
COMMENTS	This activity works best if you are working in an English-speaking country or if you have a plentiful supply of newspapers that originate from an English-speaking country. But wherever you work, your students are likely to have a sense of what their target English-speaking culture is like. Very often this is based partly on misconceptions. This activity gives you the chance to discuss the difference between the image and the reality.

2.19 News stories in two cultures

LEVEL	**Intermediate and above**
TIME	**40–50 minutes**
MATERIALS	**One current news story, access to a photocopier**
SKILLS	**Topic writing**
ACTIVITY	**How English-language and mother-tongue newspapers treat the same topic differently**

PREPARATION

Choose a contemporary news story and make a photocopy for each student. The story should be on a topic that the students will know about from mother-tongue newspapers and/or radio and television. An ideal length is 300–400 words.

PROCEDURE

1 Explain that you have brought a story with you to class. Tell the students what the topic is and spend three to four minutes discussing with them what they expect the story to say.

2 Allow 10–15 minutes for each student to write the story *in their mother tongue* just as they would expect it to appear in their own newspapers. Explain that their account should be 300–400 words in length and that it should be written on alternate lines.

3 Give out the photocopies of the story you brought with you. Ask the students to copy out all those parts of it that parallel their mother-tongue versions at the appropriate places on the intervening lines.

VARIATION

If you do not have access to a photocopier, it is still possible (although more difficult) to make this activity work. Here's how:

1 Give out newspapers and ask each student to find a current news story 300–400 words long.

2 Pair the students (check that each student in a pair has chosen a different story).

3 Ask the students to tell their partners the topics of their stories.

4 Each student now follows Stage 2 of the procedure above.

5 The students exchange the original stories with their partners. Each student copies out those parts of the original that parallel their mother-tongue versions at the appropriate places on the intervening lines.

2.20 I expected to find ... and I was surprised

LEVEL Intermediate and above

TIME Day 1—Preparation: 5 minutes in class
Day 2—Activity: 40 minutes

MATERIALS Day 1: A small piece of card for each student
Day 2: Copies of that day's newspapers

SKILLS Predicting, task-based reading

ACTIVITY Comparing newspaper and TV news presentations

PREPARATION Distribute a piece of card (a card index card, for example) to each student. Ask them to write 'I expect to find...' on one side of the card and to watch the television news in the evening.

After watching the news, each student decides on something they have seen on television that they expect to find in the next day's papers. For example, it could be a story about the Middle East or a picture of the American President looking unhappy.

Once they have decided on the likely story (or picture), the students complete their card. For example:

> *I expect to find a story about the testing of a new drug for AIDS.*

PROCEDURE 1 Collect in all the completed cards and redistribute them randomly.

2 Students should change 'expect' to 'expected', turn the cards over, and write 'and I was surprised ...'

3 Each student then takes a newspaper and completes the 'I was surprised ...' sentence.

4 Collect in all the completed cards, ask the students to sit in a circle, and redistribute them randomly.

5 Someone then reads both sides of their card. This serves as a cue to another student whose card is thematically related and in this way the class reads continuously until all the cards have been read aloud.

COMMENTS It is very surprising to discover the different prominences/emphases television and newspapers give to the same news item. This activity often gives students a rare opportunity to make their own judgements about an English-language newspaper.

2.21 Headline and story

LEVEL	**Intermediate and above**
TIME	**35–40 minutes**
MATERIALS	**At least four different newspapers published on the same day**
SKILLS	**Matching title and text, making reasoned decisions**
ACTIVITY	**Recognizing how headline and story complement each other**

PREPARATION   Cut out several different newspaper versions of the same story and remove the headlines.

PROCEDURE

1 Divide the class into as many different groups as you have different versions of the story. Write all the headlines on the board.

2 Each group studies their story and tries to decide which headline went with it.

3 After five minutes, tell the groups to pass their stories on to the next group, who then have five minutes to decide which headline went with the version now in front of them.

4 Repeat Stage 3 until all the stories have been read by each group. Reveal which headlines match which stories.

COMMENTS   The more versions you have of the same story, the better. This activity works really well when you have enough different versions to allow the students to work in pairs.

2.22 Newsvendors' posters

LEVEL	**Elementary and above**
TIME	**30–40 minutes**
MATERIALS	**One newsvendor's poster text for every three students (see Comments)**
SKILLS	**Representing the full meaning of a text**
ACTIVITY	**Studying the relationship between newsvendors' posters and newspapers**

A London newsvendor (OAPs=old age pensioners; BR=British Rail).

PROCEDURE

1 Ask the students to work in threes. Give each group the text of a different newsvendor's poster and ask them to draw an illustration of what their poster says. Each member of the group should contribute to the picture.

2 When the drawings are complete, they should be passed from group to group. Each group writes down their guess as to what the original poster said.

COMMENTS

1 Newsvendors' posters are not found in all cultures, so you may have to invent your own texts for this activity. You may also need to explain that they are very common in countries like Britain and are used as a sort of advertisement for the newspaper, with evening newspapers often having particularly sensational posters. It is easier to invent a poster when you have a newspaper in front of you. News-based poster slogans such as:

'Local murder baffles police'
'Market traders reject Council plans'

will readily occur to you.

2 Since making a collection of what is written on newsvendors' posters can take a long time, you may be able to obtain a list of recent posters from your local newspaper office. Bizarre posters are best. My favourite example is 'City boffins study Chinese wonder pigs—picture'.

3 Alternatively, if you do not live in an English-speaking country and you do sometimes see mother-tongue posters, try translating these into English.

4 If you work in an English-speaking country and collect posters over time, be sure to buy the paper each time you see a good one so that you have the story to use for follow-up work.

2.23 Three pairing techniques

LEVEL	**All levels**
TIME	**5–10 minutes for each pair activity**
MATERIALS	**A newspaper headline, adhesive labels**
SKILLS	**Matching similar words and phrases**
ACTIVITY	**Thinking about one's newspaper reading habits**
PROCEDURE	Why not use a newspaper-related idea to pair students? You can ask your students to write a word or a phrase on an adhesive label (an address label or 'post-it' will do fine). They stick this to themselves and then go to look for a partner with a matching or similar word or phrase. Here are three different ideas to try:

VARIATION 1

Ask each student to complete the sentence 'I read the newspaper ...' in a way that is true for them. For example:

I read the newspaper at breakfast time, or
I read the newspaper on the train.

VARIATION 2

Remove a word from a headline and ask the students to suggest words to replace it. They should write their suggested word on their label.

VARIATION 3

Ask the students to think of the first word that comes to mind in connection with a headline and write the word on their label.

In each case, the students stick their label to themselves and go looking for a partner with a similar phrase or word. Later it is possible to make a wall display of all the phrases or words the class has thought up.

COMMENTS

1 It is all too easy to ask students to work together just because they happen to be sitting next to each other. Students are usually much more motivated when they pair themselves with a partner with whom they have something in common.

2 If you do not have adhesive labels, get the students to write their phrase or word on a piece of paper, or even on their hands, if they agree.

3 These pairing techniques build confidence because they treat newspaper reading habits as part of the students' way of life. This may be used as a basis for grouping just as other givens like birthdays, favourite colours, or food might be used.

2.24 Story chains

LEVEL

Intermediate and above

TIME

45–50 minutes

MATERIALS

One newspaper for every three students, or your Story Bank (see page 28)

SKILLS

Identifying linking features in texts, discussion and negotiation

ACTIVITY

Making connections between newspaper stories

PROCEDURE

1 Ask the students to work in groups of five to six. Give each group a selection of newspapers or a share of your Story Bank and ask them to find and cut out 15–20 stories that interest them.

2 Once cut out, the stories should be arranged in a chain so that each one is connected in some way to the one before and the one after. The connection may be a name in common, a vocabulary item, something thematic—anything the students agree on.

3 Ask two groups to come together and explain their story chains to each other.

VARIATION

At Stage 3, you can ask the groups to study each others' chains and try and guess some of the connections. This is difficult and time consuming.

COMMENTS

This activity makes it necessary for the students to read each story and agree on a rationale for the way the stories are linked. This involves a good deal of negotiation and decision making.

2.25 The panel

LEVEL

Intermediate and above

TIME

Preparation time: see below
Activity: 20–30 minutes

MATERIALS

That day's newspapers—if possible two complete sets

SKILLS

Task reading, question and answer techniques, contributing to public discussion

ACTIVITY

Deciding how to follow up reading with discussion

PREPARATION

1 Ask the class to choose three or four students to go on a panel to answer questions about an item in the news the following day.

2 The next day, give the panel the day's newspapers and ask them to decide which major story they want to be asked about. Once they have chosen their story, give them an hour to read all the newspaper treatments of it and think about what they might want to say about it themselves. The rest of the class will need to be involved in a different activity for the first 40 minutes of this hour.

3 After the panel has been at work for 40 minutes, give out newspapers to the rest of the class. Tell the students which story the panel will take questions on. Allow 20 minutes for each student to decide on and write down at least one question they would like to ask.

PROCEDURE

Ask the class to choose a Chairperson to run the panel. Allow 20–30 minutes for questions to the panel.

COMMENTS	You do not actually need English-language newspapers for this activity as long as the questions and the panel discussion are in English.

Acknowledgement
This is John Morgan's idea.

2.26 Matching comment and newspaper

LEVEL	**Intermediate and above**
TIME	**40 minutes**
MATERIALS	**One newspaper for every two students. You must have a variety of newspapers.**
SKILLS	**Evaluation of written materials, group decision-making**
ACTIVITY	**Making judgements about newspapers**
PREPARATION	Write up the following list of comments on the board:

no thank you	ideal for a desert island
mind your own business	a big yawn
sensational	not sure about this one
six out of ten	boring but worthy
a great read	very mixed
not enough variety	who said newspapers were dull?

PROCEDURE	1 Ask the students to work in groups of five to six. Give each group three or four different newspapers. Each group studies its newspapers and tries to allocate each of the comments on the board to a newspaper.
	2 If you wish, two groups can then combine and share their results. The combined group can now decide which comment fits which paper most accurately.
COMMENTS	This activity leads to a surprisingly detailed and varied examination of the contents of the newspapers each group works with. The more different titles you have, the better this activity works. So it is best to have several different English-language newspapers readily available.

2.27 The stories I would like to read

LEVEL Upper-intermediate and above

TIME 40 minutes

MATERIALS One newspaper for every five students, or your Story Bank (see page 28)

SKILLS Identifying a theme, authentic reading

ACTIVITY Deciding which stories to read and which to skip

PROCEDURE 1 Give out newspapers or make your Story Bank available. Ask each student to find a story that interests them.

2 Each student looks for the single most significant word in the story: this word will probably give an idea of what the story is about. The significant word should be written down on a separate sheet of paper. Under it each student lists every other word in the story which begins with the same letter as the significant word.

3 Each student displays their word list (but not their story) on their desk. The students circulate and sign their names under the word lists of the four stories they would most like to read.

4 The students then return to their desks and display their stories alongside their word lists. They circulate again, reading the four stories they had signed up for.

COMMENTS We are all discriminating about what we read in the newspapers. Learning to be equally discriminating with foreign-language newspapers is to acquire an authentic reading skill in the foreign language.

2.28 Reviews

LEVEL Upper-elementary and above

TIME 25–30 minutes

MATERIALS One newspaper for every five students

SKILLS Controlled writing

ACTIVITY Assessing the type and quality of a newspaper

PROCEDURE Ask the students to work in groups of four to five. Give each group a newspaper and ask them to review it in *exactly* 40 words, neither fewer nor more. The review should indicate how suitable the newspaper is for language learners.

VARIATION

If you do not have a regular supply of English-language newspapers, try using the extracts from English-language newspapers that you can find in coursebooks.

COMMENTS

This activity helps learners to discriminate between one newspaper and another. It works best in classes where you are working regularly with a range of daily papers, and particularly well at some stage in a week's project on newspapers. It also prepares the students for buying their own English-language newspapers.

2.29 Buying newspapers

LEVEL

Upper-elementary and above

TIME

15–20 minutes, preferably at the end of a lesson

MATERIALS

One piece of card for each student

SKILLS

Working with double meanings and riddles

ACTIVITY

Getting the students to buy a newspaper

PREPARATION

Prepare one small piece of card for each student.

PROCEDURE

How do you get your students to buy an English-language newspaper to bring to class when you need this resource? Here is a suggestion:

1 Ask the students to make a list of all the English-language newspapers available locally. Check that this is complete, or at least contains all the newspapers you want the students to buy.

2 Give the students a small piece of card each and ask them to write down on it the name of one of the newspapers on their list. Make sure that all the available newspapers are more or less equally represented.

3 On the other side of the card each learner should write a riddle whose solution is the name of the paper written on the front. For example:
'It shines on you every day'—the *Sun*
'You can see yourself in it'—the *Daily Mirror*

4 The students circulate, trying to guess each other's riddles. When both members of a pair guess correctly, they exchange cards.

5 When you judge it appropriate, stop the activity and tell the students to buy the paper indicated on the cards they are holding at that moment.

VARIATION

The cards can be used up to three days running. On the fourth day, tell the students to buy the paper of their choice—you will be surprised how positive they are.

COMMENT

This activity only works where there is a range of English-speaking newspapers available.

2.30 Reading your own paper

LEVEL

Upper-elementary and above

TIME

45 minutes

MATERIALS

One newspaper for each student

SKILLS

Selective reading and comparing

ACTIVITY

Authentic newspaper reading

PROCEDURE

1 Ask each student to spend 10 minutes imagining they have just 20 minutes to skim through their favourite mother-tongue daily newspaper. They should note down which parts of the paper they would look at, in which order, and how long they would spend on each.

2 Give out an English-language newspaper to each student and ask them to spend 20 minutes doing exactly as they would with their favourite mother-tongue newspaper.

3 Set aside 10–15 minutes for a discussion of the differences the students have noticed between the mother-tongue and the English-language newspapers.

COMMENTS

Because this activity requires one newspaper for each student, it may be an ideal time to ask the students to buy and bring to class their own English-language newspaper. Buying one's own foreign-language newspaper is a very important psychological step, which this activity makes much less daunting. Once this has been achieved, you can use each student's newspaper for several other activities, thus giving the students the sense that they really have got their money's worth and that they know their own newspaper inside out.

3 Working with texts

This chapter does not contain any of the well-known comprehension activities that are usually applied to newspaper materials. Instead, the text-based activities in this chapter usually require extensive, discriminating, authentic reading.

There are inevitably some practical difficulties involved in working with texts. For example, a number of the activities are easier to use when you have access to a photocopier and can make multiple copies of a text (although there is always a photocopier-free variation in this chapter). Two or three of the activities only work when you have a set of a single day's newspapers, and therefore if you are teaching where a range of English-language newspapers is not available, these are not for you. Nevertheless, the majority of the 22 activities in this chapter are simple to use and require only a Story Bank (see page 28) or the odd newspaper.

The activities fall into four broad categories: reading for information (activities 3.1 and 3.2), style or text-type analysis (activities 3.3–3.8), classifying and categorizing texts (activities 3.9–3.18), and activities where the students contribute to the text (3.19–3.22).

3.1 Matching story and summary

LEVEL

Upper-elementary and above

TIME

45 minutes

MATERIALS

Story Bank (see page 28)

SKILLS

Summarizing, matching outline and text

ACTIVITY

Separating the essential from the inessential in newspaper stories

PROCEDURE

1 Ask each student to take a story from your Story Bank, read it, and write a *three-sentence* summary of it.

2 Ask the students to display their stories on the wall. Collect in the summaries and redistribute them round the class so that each student gets someone else's.

3 Each student tries to match the summary they have been given with the story on which it was based.

VARIATION 1

As well as writing a three-sentence summary, get each student to include a fourth sentence which makes sense in relation to the other three but which has nothing to do with the story. After the students have matched story and summary, they cross out the sentence which has nothing to do with the story.

VARIATION 2

Ask each student to put their name on their summary. After Stage 3, each student finds the summary writer and tells them how they might have done a better job.

COMMENTS

The students only realise the skills required in good summary writing when they try to find the original story on which the summary they were given was based.

3.2 Same name, no relative

LEVEL

Intermediate and above

TIME

40–45 minutes

MATERIALS

One newspaper for every four students or your Story Bank (see page 28), glue

SKILLS

Task reading, creative thinking

ACTIVITY

Finding out the extent to which ordinary people feature in newspapers

PROCEDURE

1 Ask the students to work in groups of three to four. Hand out a newspaper to each group or make your Story Bank available. Ask the group to spend 20 minutes looking for and cutting out as many stories as they can find about ordinary people with the same same surname as famous people.

2 Tell the groups they have 10 minutes to decide what family relation the ordinary person in each of their stories has to the famous person. For example, 'brother who made a lot of money in a doubtful way', 'disreputable aunt', 'sister who married a foreigner', 'illegitimate offspring', 'uncle who's never mentioned', etc.

3 The stories should be glued to sheets of paper and the relationship of the person in the story and their famous namesake indicated.

4 The sheets of paper should be displayed on the wall. Allow 10–15 minutes' reading time.

COMMENTS

This is a fun activity which motivates careful reading both initially and at the wall display stage.

3.3 The short, short story

LEVEL

Elementary and above

TIME

30–40 minutes

MATERIALS

One newspaper for every five students, or your Story Bank (see page 28)

SKILLS

Asking and answering questions appropriately

ACTIVITY

Studying newspaper 'snippets'

PREPARATION

If you are using your Story Bank, select only the very short stories. You may have to supplement your store of this sort of story for this activity.

PROCEDURE

1 Give out newspapers or make your Story Bank available. Ask the students to find and cut out a very short story, preferably a human interest or local culture one. (This makes a good homework activity if the students have access to newspapers outside class.)

2 Ask the students to work in groups of four to five. They try to guess each others' stories in turn by asking 'yes/no' questions, such as: 'Is it a crime story?', 'Is it a sports story?', 'Is it about an animal?', 'Is there a policeman in the story?', etc.

VARIATION

After you have done this activity two or three times, ask the students to write a few short, short stories of their own.

COMMENTS

1 If your class is not used to this sort of activity, it is usually a good idea to demonstrate by bringing your own short story to class first for the students to try and guess. For example, you could demonstrate with the following articles:

A cure for cancer?

Scientists working in Japan have discovered that ink produced by cuttlefish may help to cure cancer. 60 per cent of mice tested with the ink recovered from tumours.

Dumb mistake

Police divers searched a river in Witney, Oxfordshire yester-day after a passer-by reported seeing a body. After three hours they recovered a tailor's dummy.

Egg on his face

A student who threw an egg at the Prime Minister during a visit to Nottingham has been fined £100 and ordered to pay £10 towards cleaning his victim's suit.

Caught red-handed

A gang of robbers used a fork-lift truck to try and steal a cash-point machine yesterday. They rammed the truck into the window of the building society and dug out the machine, but were arrested before they could escape with the cash.

It's a dog's life

Redundant shepherds are pressing for unemployment benefits to be paid for their sheepdogs. They say the dogs are necessary for their work, but may have to be put down if they cannot afford to feed them.

Bees banned

Bees in south-west England have been forbidden to travel north due to an outbreak of the disease varroasis. A spokesman for the Beekeepers' Federation said the ban was 'impractical'.

Slow food

Travellers on British Rail's delayed six o'clock train from London to Edinburgh received a pleasant surprise yesterday. They were given free sandwiches from the buffet. The only snag—the train was so slow that the sandwiches had passed the sell-by date!

Cave rescue

Two stranded potholers were found last night after a 30-hour search in a cave under the Peak District in Derbyshire. A rescue worker described the caves as an "endless labyrinth".

2 The students can learn a great deal about the local culture in a very short time from working with these revealing stories.

3.4 Separating news and comment

LEVEL	**Upper-intermediate and above**
TIME	**30–45 minutes**
MATERIALS	**Political stories (see Preparation and Comments), glue**
SKILLS	**Identifying implied meaning and partisan writing**
ACTIVITY	**Raising awareness of bias in political writing**
PREPARATION	Cut out one political story for every two students.
PROCEDURE	**1** Pair the students and give each pair a political story. They should either underline or highlight only those sentences in it that are entirely objective and give no hint of the attitude of the writer. For example, 'Euromania haunts language of food' would therefore look like this:

Euromania haunts language of food

From GEORGE BROCK
IN BRUSSELS

EUROCRATS are trying to interfere with the hallowed language of food. Outraged members of the European Parliament have told them to stop rewriting the law on which sprouts can be called Brussels sprouts.

Ken Collins, Labour MEP for Strathclyde East, has asked the European Commission to withdraw a proposal which would require eccles cakes to come from Eccles, the Brussels sprout to come only from the Belgian capital and hamburgers to hail from Hamburg. He describes the draft regulation on the "protection of geographical indications and designations of origin" as "meddlesome, unworkable and unnecessary".

In a clumsy attempt to tell consumers about the quality of a product the commission has proposed that any product containing a placename should be "produced or processed in the corresponding geographical area". Mr Collins' splendidly indignant polemic on behalf of Dundee cake and Peking duck explains why the regulation would be unworkable. Limiting himself only to English usage, he lists cakes from Eccles, Dundee and Pontefract, frankfurters and Yorkshire pudding. "Is the commission seriously suggesting," he writes, "that in future they can only retain these names if produced in the places whose name they bear?"

The planned edict in the use of generic names is an attempt at thought control, Mr Collins says. "If people

choose to call a particular pastry filled with meat, potato and carrots a 'Cornish pasty', this is because they find it simple and convenient to do so. You cannot control this process by legislation."

Sometimes, however, Jacques Delors, president of the commission, must wonder if he can ever succeed in pleasing anybody. He is now in trouble with the European Parliament's animal welfare group for refusing to *extend* community laws to Europe's 1,000 zoos. The commission has been discussing suggestions that the community should lay down minimum welfare and safety standards for zoos for a couple of years. But M Delors and one of the German commissioners have now stalled the idea on the grounds that the issue should be left to national governments.

2 The story should be glued on a large sheet of paper. Ask the students to copy all the sentences that are not highlighted on to the sheet immediately below the story. They should circle those parts of the sentences they have copied which reveal the writer's attitude. In 'Euromania haunts language of food', for example, the first sentence copied would therefore look like this:

Eurocrats are (trying to interfere) with the (hallowed) language of food.

COMMENTS

1 Make sure that you choose suitable stories otherwise some pairs will have much more work to do than others.

2 This is a very revealing activity. It gives the students the sense that they can really understand two different functions of English and identify those features that reveal partisan writing.

3.5 Why the headline?

LEVEL — Intermediate and above

TIME — 35–40 minutes

MATERIALS — One story for every five students, access to photocopier

SKILLS — Writing and evaluating definitions, explaining double meanings in clear English

ACTIVITY — Understanding headlines and how they relate to stories

PREPARATION   Choose one story for every six students from your Story Bank (see page 28). The stories you choose must have interesting headlines, preferably with double meanings. Make enough copies for each pair of students to get one of the stories. So if there are 30 students in the class, you will choose five stories and make three copies of each.

PROCEDURE   1 Pair the students and give each pair a story. They should read it and then, without quoting the headline, write a short explanation of why the headline was chosen. For example, if a pair received 'Euromania haunts the language of food' (see page 59), they might write something like:

> The headline shows that the European Commission wants to change the name of some kinds of food which are named after a place (for example, Brussels sprout).

It is usually a good idea to demonstrate what is required with an example like this.

2 Group the students according to which story they worked on. Ask each group to exchange their story and headline explanations with another group. Each group then decides which of the explanations they have received is the most accurate.

VARIATION 1   This activity is still possible without a photocopier, but it takes a little longer. Here's how:

1 Group the students in sixes and ask each group to separate into three pairs. Give each pair a suitable story.

2 The three pairs in each group of six independently study each story and write a headline explanation for it.

3 Each group of six exchanges their three stories and headline explanations with another group. Each group then decides which of the explanations is most accurate.

VARIATION 2   A much more difficult variation which really advanced students sometimes enjoy is trying to reconstruct the original headlines from headline explanations like that given in Stage 1 of the Procedure for this activity.

COMMENTS   This is a more difficult writing task than may at first appear to be the case. The writer has to reveal the meaning of a few carefully chosen, very economical words and at the same time the explanation must relate accurately to the substantial text that follows.

3.6 Which writer?

LEVEL	**Upper-intermediate and above**
TIME	**20–25 minutes**
MATERIALS	**Story Bank (see page 28)**
SKILLS	**Looking at authors' styles**
ACTIVITY	**Investigating whether different story types are written in different styles**

PREPARATION Make four piles of stories from your Story Bank. Each pile should contain a different type of story. For example, Pile 1 might contain popular press news stories, Pile 2 quality press news stories, Pile 3 feature articles, and Pile 4 stories about ordinary people.

PROCEDURE 1 Group the students in threes and ask each group to take a story from each of the four piles.

2 Ask each group to imagine that their four different stories were written by three different journalists. Each group should now decide which two were written by the same author, and justify their choice.

3 Ask groups to combine and share their decisions.

COMMENTS This activity helps the students to look more objectively at both subject matter and writing style. Often the reasons students give for deciding which articles have a common author are the starting point for a more detailed examination of the texts.

3.7 How original is the language?

LEVEL	**Intermediate and above**
TIME	**30–40 minutes**
MATERIALS	**One colourful story, access to a photocopier**
SKILLS	**Distinguishing original language and cliché**
ACTIVITY	**Discovering to what extent newspapers use cliché and original language**

PREPARATION Choose a colourful story—sensational stories from a popular newspapers work well. Make a copy. Circle all the clichés you can find on the copy. If you are not a native speaker, you may find a native speaker helpful at this stage. Make a copy of the original and of the copy with clichés marked for each student in the class.

PROCEDURE

1 Give out the unmarked copies and ask each student to underline all the original, colourful language they can find in the story.

2 When everyone has done this, give out the copies with clichés marked and ask the students to discuss the texts in small groups.

Ban on migrant cheats

NEW laws to protect Britain from a tidal wave of illegal immigrants will be rushed through at breakneck speed.

Ministers fear a deluge of bogus applications for political asylum from people seeking an easy life in the UK.

Experts believe seven million people in the crisis-torn former Soviet empire plan to flood into western Europe.

Proposed measures include finger-printing asylum-seekers to prevent benefits fraud and to stop cheats

sneaking back under false names.

The automatic right of some asylum-seekers to get free homes from local councils will be scrapped. And appeal hearings, which can allow cheats to stay for years before being booted out, will be speeded up.

Extra staff will be taken on at airports and ferryports to halt bogus refugees. But the government will vow full protection for genuine asylum-seekers fleeing torture or persecution.

COMMENTS

This activity works because very often what seems colourful and original to a non-native speaker is thought of as a cliché by a native speaker. Finding this out helps learners to see that they may have perceptions about the target language which are not shared by those who are more familiar with it.

VARIATION 1

If native speakers are available to help, ask them to come into class and work with three or four students. The students mark the original, colourful language and the native speakers mark the clichés, and then they talk about it together.

VARIATION 2

You can try other experiments of this sort. For example, a native member of the culture will react differently to particular stories from a non-native member. Or the men and women in a class may find different parts of a newspaper more appealing—do they read the sections (often thought of as) aimed at the other sex?

VARIATION 3

It is very difficult to do this activity without the use of a photocopier. Variation 1 can be done without a photocopier provided that the students and the native speakers each have a copy of the same story. If you buy two copies of the same popular paper, you may find four or five stories suitable for this activity in them.

Acknowledgement
The original idea is John Morgan's.

3.8 Grading for difficulty

LEVEL

Intermediate and above

TIME

At least 60 minutes

MATERIALS

One newspaper for every three students, or your Story Bank (see page 28)

SKILLS

Analysing comprehension problems

ACTIVITY

Assessing the readability of newspaper stories

PROCEDURE

1 Group the students in threes and distribute one newspaper to each group or make your Story Bank available. Allow the group 10 minutes to chose four different stories to work on—an international story, a local story, a sports story, and a feature article.

2 Allow a further 20 minutes while the groups grade their stories from most difficult to least difficult to understand.

3 Ask the whole class to brainstorm reasons why one story might be more difficult to understand than another.

4 Once you have five or six convincing reasons (such as too many new words, too many long words, long sentences, new subject matter, unknown people, implies prior knowledge which the reader has not got, not logically constructed), allow 30–40 minutes for each group to score each of their four stories for each of these criteria.

5 Hold a short whole class discussion to find out which of the imagined criteria for difficulty actually turned up in the stories. Did they discover any other reasons that might account for why one story was more difficult than another? Does each group still put its four stories in the same order?

COMMENTS

This activity almost assumes project proportions. It can easily be expanded to become at least a half-day project on grading stories for readability both across types of story, as here, and within a single category, such as the sports story. Handled in the right way, projects on story difficulty increase students' confidence by enabling them to make judgements. They also often lead to wonderful wall displays where one can arrange materials from 'readable' to 'unreadable'.

3.9 Finding stories

LEVEL	**Intermediate and above**
TIME	**15–20 minutes**
MATERIALS	**One newspaper for every five students, or your Story Bank (see page 28)**
SKILLS	**Reading for meaning**
ACTIVITY	**Categorizing stories by type**

PROCEDURE   Give out newspapers or make your Story Bank available and ask the students to find a story of a particular type. Types you can use include silly stories, animal stories, xenophobic stories, unlikely stories, stories about mothers-in-law, teachers, priests, etc., stories that make you angry, funny stories, sad stories, stories about your country, love stories.

COMMENTS   This is a well-known idea, but it is included here just in case you have not tried it before. Once the students have found a story of the type set, there are all sorts of activities you can do with it. For example:

- the stories can be graded from best to worst example of the type;
- the class, or groups within the class, can start a collection of one type of story—eventually this will lead to sub-types within the same overall category;
- the students can plan (and write) a pastiche. This works well for animal and xenophobic stories in particular;
- a story can be rewritten so that it changes category: a love story might become a xenophobic story, for example.

3.10 Enough is enough

LEVEL	**Intermediate and above**
TIME	**Student preparation + up to 35 minutes in class**
MATERIALS	**One story per student**
SKILLS	**Rapid authentic reading, reading for choice, self-monitoring, and reading**
ACTIVITY	**Learning when an English-language newspaper is too boring to be worth reading**

PREPARATION

Students
As a homework activity, ask students each to choose one story they find interesting from the day's papers and bring it to class the following morning. Alternatively, this can be done in class.

PROCEDURE

1 Ask the students to display the stories on the wall or on their desks.

2 Tell the students they have just as many minutes as there are stories (30 minutes where there are more than 30 stories) in which to circulate and read as many of the stories as possible. Although they should try to read everything, they will only have time to read the most interesting stories all the way through. They should therefore read each story only up to the point where they are no longer interested, and then make a mark where they stopped reading or skipped to the end.

VARIATION 1

After the time allocated is up, the stories can be arranged from most marked (i.e. least interesting) to least marked (i.e. most interesting). This can lead to a discussion as to what makes a story interesting or boring.

VARIATION 2

The student homework is a good idea as the pride of ownership is important in this activity. Each student needs to discover whether they have chosen a story which is to the taste of other readers. But if this is difficult, you can always supply newspapers or your Story Bank (see page 28) and ask the students to select a story.

COMMENTS

You will almost certainly find that the students read very quickly in this activity and do not need all the time you allow. They will be surprised at how fast they can read given the right stimulus.

3.11 Rejects

LEVEL

Intermediate and above

TIME

30 minutes

MATERIALS

Story Bank (see page 28)

SKILLS

Finding reasons to support decisions, re-thinking decisions

ACTIVITY

Discriminating between newspaper contents

PROCEDURE

1 The students may work individually or in pairs. Take your Story Bank to class and give out eight stories to each pair/ individual and ask them to spend 10 minutes reading them and

dividing them into two piles: those they would be happy to work with, and those they do not want to work with.

2 Collect in all the stories the students are happy to work with.

3 Ask the students to decide precisely why they rejected the stories they did. Were they right, or can they now find something interesting in each of their rejected stories?

VARIATION 1

Business English students often ask to practise 'small talk'. At Stage 3, can they find suitable small talk subject-matter in the stories they initially rejected?

VARIATION 2

Make photocopies of the same eight stories and give each individual/pair a set of the photocopied stories at Stage 1. After Stage 3, ask the students to form small groups and compare their decisions: which stories did each pair/group reject and which did they rehabilitate? Allow an extra 15 minutes for this variation.

COMMENTS

This activity also works well as a teacher training activity which you could try in a training session with your colleagues: it obliges you to look again at materials you would instinctively reject. And it often turns out to be the case that different teachers reject different materials—you can demonstrate this by asking each teacher in a pair to reject stories individually before sharing their decisions with each other.

3.12 Same theme, different treatments

LEVEL

Intermediate and above

TIME

30–40 minutes

MATERIALS

One newspaper for every four students, or your Story Bank (see page 28)

SKILLS

Reading judgementally, recognizing partial similarity

ACTIVITY

Discovering the variety of newspaper treatments of a single topic

PROCEDURE

1 Pair the students and give out newspapers or make your Story Bank available. Each pair tries to find several pairs of stories which treat the same theme in different ways. For example, a sensational description of a football match might be paired with a considered article about the prospects of a team in a future competition. Each 'pair' should be displayed on the wall.

2 Allow 10 minutes' reading time during which the students decide which pair of stories they particularly like, or which pairing seems particularly striking.

COMMENTS

In learning a language it is very important to remember that similarity and difference are not such simple notions as we sometimes think. Nor are particular themes treated in one single style, although we sometimes forget this.

3.13 Reconstructing stories

LEVEL

Intermediate and above

TIME

30–40 minutes

MATERIALS

Two versions of the same story, access to a photocopier, glue

SKILLS

Matching texts written in a common style

ACTIVITY

Discovering how story contents are structured

PREPARATION

Choose a story which appears in two different newspapers. If the two newspapers have the same typeface, this is even better. Separate each paragraph in each of the stories. Glue them in random order on a single sheet of paper and make photocopies for each student. For example, from 'He's too Cosi with my girl' and 'Opera star confronted by leading lady's boyfriend':

He's too Cosi with my girl

By SUZANNE O'SHEA

PASSION and jealousy spilled over into real life after a rehearsal for the posh Glyndebourne opera.

Humble chorus singer David Ellis watched in the wings as girlfriend Amanda Roocroft's embrace with star Kurt Streit lingered a little too long.

The grand finale came at an opening party for Cosi fan tutte—Mozart's masterpiece about unfaithful women and jealous men.

Ellis punched the hunky American tenor when he kissed 26-year-old Amanda farewell at the restaurant party in Nether Wallop.

Streit took a bow — to the casualty department at Lewes Hospital, Sussex.

Yesterday he was recovering from bruised ribs and a cut eye. Ellis was moved to another opera.

But the show goes on. Cosi fan tutte opens tonight . . . with Streit and blonde soprano Amanda gazing adoringly into each other's eyes for another 13 performances.

Opera star confronted by leading lady's boyfriend

KURT STREIT, the American tenor, needed stitches to his face after he allegedly became too friendly with his leading lady and her boyfriend hit him, it was disclosed yesterday.

Mr Streit, who plays Ferrando in Trevor Nunn's Glyndebourne production of Mozart's *Cosi Fan Tutte*, embraced the soprano Amanda Roocroft, 24, who plays Fiordiligi, as part of the plot.

But her boyfriend, David Ellis, 22, a singer in the chorus line who was watching from the wings, apparently felt that his wooing was much too bravura. A confrontation with Mr Streit during the after-show party at the Nether Wallop Restaurant ended in blows.

A Glyndebourne spokeswoman, Helen O'Neil, said last night: "It is all completely over now. Apologies have been offered and accepted on both sides and Kurt Streit has not missed a single performance. All he had was a tiny cut on his cheekbone, it was nothing."

Mr Nunn said he knew nothing of the confrontation, and Glyndebourne owner, Sir George Christie, refused to comment on the incident, which happened last Friday.

The Royal Sussex County Hospital in Brighton said Mr Streit was admitted to the hospital's accident and emergency department and later discharged, but could not confirm whether he received stitches.

you might make up the following sheet:

PASSION and jealousy spilled over into real life after a rehearsal for the posh Glyndebourne opera.

Streit took a bow — to the casualty department at Lewes Hospital, Sussex.

A Glyndebourne spokeswoman, Helen O'Neil, said last night: "It is all completely over now. Apologies have been offered and accepted on both sides and Kurt Streit has not missed a single performance. All he had was a tiny cut on his cheekbone, it was nothing."

Mr Streit, who plays Ferrando in Trevor Nunn's Glyndebourne production of Mozart's *Cosi Fan Tutte*, embraced the soprano Amanda Roocroft, 24, who plays Fiordiligi, as part of the plot.

Ellis punched the hunky American tenor when he kissed 26-year-old Amanda farewell at the restaurant party in Nether Wallop.

KURT STREIT, the American tenor, needed stitches to his face after he allegedly became too friendly with his leading lady and her boyfriend hit him, it was disclosed yesterday.

Humble chorus singer David Ellis watched in the wings as girlfriend Amanda Roocroft's embrace with star Kurt Streit lingered a little too long.

But her boyfriend, David Ellis, 22, a singer in the chorus line who was watching from the wings, apparently felt that his wooing was much too bravura. A confrontation with Mr Streit during the after-show party at the Nether Wallop Restaurant ended in blows.

The Royal Sussex County Hospital in Brighton said Mr Streit was admitted to the hospital's accident and emergency department and later discharged, but could not confirm whether he received stitches.

Yesterday he was recovering from bruised ribs and a cut eye. Ellis was moved to another opera.

The grand finale came at an opening party for Cosi fan tutte— Mozart's masterpiece about unfaithful women and jealous men.

But the show goes on. Cosi fan tutte opens tonight . . . with Streit and blonde soprano Amanda gazing adoringly into each other's eyes for another 13 performances.

Mr Nunn said he knew nothing of the confrontation, and Glyndebourne owner, Sir George Christie, refused to comment on the incident, which happened last Friday.

PROCEDURE

1 Pair the students, give out the photocopies and ask them to reconstruct each of the two stories.

2 When you reveal the solution, allow a few minutes for small group or even whole class discussion. This discussion should centre on whether the student versions make more or less sense than the actual one.

VARIATION

If you do not have access to a photocopier, one option is to distribute newspapers and ask each pair of students to find their own pair of stories to prepare for another pair to reconstruct. You can also save pairs of stories from old newspapers and use them for this activity.

3.14 Identical and fraternal twins

LEVEL

Intermediate and above

TIME

40–60 minutes

MATERIALS

A full set of newspapers from the same day

SKILLS

Extensive reading, making exact judgements about comparable texts

ACTIVITY

Comparing degrees of similarity and difference in treatments of the same story

PROCEDURE

1 Ask the students to work in pairs. Give out newspapers and ask each pair to find two versions of one story which are as alike as possible.

2 Very similar versions are 'identical' twins and broadly similar are 'fraternal' twins—designate an 'identical' and a 'fraternal' wall for display.

3 Allow 10 minutes' reading time.

COMMENTS

1 This activity requires each student to read extensively. One newspaper must be carefully scanned and then several others scanned more rapidly to find stories that twin.

2 Because this exercise depends on a set of newspapers for a single day, it is only possible in English-speaking countries or where a range of newspapers is readily available. If you do not have these available, you could work instead with the 'identical twins' given in the Variation below.

VARIATION

In Britain, stories are frequently obtained from agencies and appear in very similar forms in different newspapers. These stories can also be used for detailed text-based follow-up work. For example, you could ask your students to make a list of everything they can find in each of the following 'identical twins' that does not occur in the other:

BIBLE BASHER!

RELIGIOUS freak Robin Baker was jailed yesterday — for bashing his girlfriend black and blue with a bag of BIBLES.

He beat up lover with Good Books

Jehovah's Witness Baker flew into an unholy rage when Susan Downes complained he was playing records too loudly.

He lashed out with the bag of Good Books— sending divorcee Susan sprawling to the ground.

Then he dragged her along the floor by the hair and kicked and punched her all over the body, shouting: *"It's the devil in you"* and *"Satan's got a hold of you."*

Terrified Susan was only saved from further punishment when her screams of pain woke her 13-year-old daughter Sasha.

The brave teenager punched 34-year-old Baker before she and her mother locked themselves in a room and escaped through a window.

By MARTIN STOTE

Prosecutor David Price told Leicester Crown Court that Baker had drunk five pints in a pub before the attack in Susan's home.

Baker — who told police he attended church three or four times a week — went berserk when she complained about the loud music.

Susan suffered cuts and bruises to her face and body and lost some hair during the vicious ten-minute beating.

Ripped

Her ear was also injured when Baker ripped an earring from it.

Mr. Price said Baker *later told police he was deeply in love with Susan — to the point of being obsessed with her.*

Baker, of Kimberley Road, Leicester, was jailed for a year after admitting assault causing actual bodily harm.

Judge Christopher Young told Baker: "Mrs. Downes had given you her friendship and the hospitality of her home.

"Yet you repaid her with this assault over a trivial matter."

It is the second time Baker has been in trouble for attacking a woman.

Last year he was ordered to do 120 hours of community service after assaulting a disabled woman near his home.

BIBLE-BASHER!

Lovesick Robin yells 'Satan has you' as he hits girl with bag full of Bibles

By JOHN ASKILL

RELIGIOUS nut Robin Baker was jailed for assault yesterday — after bashing his girl-friend with a carrier bag full of bibles.

As he attacked attractive divorcee Susan Downes, the lovesick Jehovah's Witness yelled: "It's the Devil in you ... Satan's got a hold of you," a court heard.

Baker, who told police he loved Mrs Downes "to the point of ob-session," **KNOCKED** her down with the Bibles, **DRAGGED** her by the hair, **PUNCHED** and **KICKED** her.

The attack came after Mrs Downes, 33, poked fun at his beliefs and ordered him to leave her home for playing records too loud, Leicester Crown Court heard.

She was saved because her screams woke her daughter, Sasha, 13, who punched Baker.

Prosecutor Mr David Price said that Mrs Downes suffered cuts and bruises and was also injured when Baker, 34, ripped off one of her earrings.

He said Baker, a jobless gardener who went to church three times a week, had known Mrs Downes, of Mere Road, Leicester, for several years. She said the relationship was "platonic."

Baker, of Leicester, who had five pints of beer before calling at Mrs Downes' home at 11pm, admitted assault causing actual bodily harm and was jailed for a year.

Last August, he was sentenced to 120 hours community service for assaulting a disabled woman in a row over an iron.

3.15 One story, many versions

LEVEL	**Intermediate and above**
TIME	**60 minutes**
MATERIALS	**One complete set of the same day's newspapers for every 12 students—that day's if possible**
SKILLS	**Differentiating pieces of writing**
ACTIVITY	**Identifying the attributes of particular newspapers and stories**
PROCEDURE	**1** Ask the students to work in groups of five to seven. Place the newspapers on a table in the middle of the classroom. Explain that each group may take up to three at a time.

2 Each group first chooses a story and then cuts out all the different versions of it from the various newspapers. Make sure that each group chooses a different story.

3 Ask the groups to find as many ways of classifying the versions as there are versions (i.e. eight versions will lead to eight ways of classifying them), so that each version will be the best according to some criterion (for example, most informative, most human, funniest, most detailed, most sensational, most boring).

4 Ask the groups to share their decisions with the class.

VARIATION 1

It is also possible to make up a 'very best' version using pictures, headlines, sub-headings, and text from the various versions. Part of the fun of doing this is making decisions about layout.

VARIATION 2

You can also place more emphasis on the sharing of decisions stage (Stage 4) by turning it into a kind of newspaper review. Some newspapers turn out to be consistently informative and detailed whatever the story whilst others are consistently superficial or sensational.

COMMENTS

1 Intermediate students may have difficulties with this activity, but if you have a group with some upper-intermediate or advanced students too, it works fine.

2 As you need a complete or nearly complete set of one day's newspapers, this activity is easiest in an English-speaking country.

3.16 Stories and headlines 1

LEVEL

Intermediate and above

TIME

60 minutes

MATERIALS

Headlines, Story Bank (see page 28)

SKILLS

Reading and classifying

ACTIVITY

Discovering the extent to which a headline is story specific

PREPARATION

Cut out 15–20 headlines. Try to choose fairly general headlines such as 'Would you believe it?' rather than very specific ones like 'Maradona the greatest, says Gazza'.

PROCEDURE

1 Display the headlines on the wall and ask each student to take a story from your Story Bank and display it on the wall under the most appropriate headline. If there are no appropriate headlines, the story should be returned.

2 Continue this process until all the stories you brought into class are under appropriate headlines.

3 Suggest that each student chooses a single headline and reads the stories displayed under it.

3.17 Stories and headlines 2

LEVEL	**Intermediate and above**
TIME	**30 minutes per story**
MATERIALS	**Headlines, Story Bank (see page 28)**
SKILLS	**Assessing headlines**
ACTIVITY	**Discovering the extent to which a headline is story specific**

PREPARATION Cut out 15–20 headlines. Try to choose fairly general headlines such as 'Would you believe it?' rather than very specific ones like 'Maradonna the greatest, says Gazza'.

PROCEDURE 1 Display the headlines on the wall and ask each student to take a story from your Story Bank, read it, and list under it all the headlines that fit the story. The headlines should be listed in order from most to least appropriate.

2 This process may be repeated as often as appropriate.

3.18 Exaggeration and inaccuracy

LEVEL	**Intermediate and above**
TIME	**30 minutes**
MATERIALS	**Four or five different newspapers for the same day**
SKILLS	**Comparing and evaluating texts**
ACTIVITY	**Discovering to what extent newspapers respect accuracy and truth**

PROCEDURE Ask the students to work in pairs or threes. Give out newspapers and ask each group to find two versions of the same story from different newspapers and decide which parts of each story are credible and which are less credible, by looking at which version includes which elements of the story.

VARIATIONS Other possibilities include comparing two versions for informativeness, clarity, interest, warmth, entertainment value, etc. Some of these variations are suitable for students on the elementary/intermediate boundary too.

3.19 Fleshing stories out

LEVEL

Upper-elementary and above

TIME

35–40 minutes

MATERIALS

One human interest story, access to a photocopier

SKILLS

Writing in a certain style

ACTIVITY

Considering appropriate contents for newspaper stories

PREPARATION

Choose a human interest story about ordinary people and make one copy for every four students in the class. Make sure that there are wide margins on the copy.

PROCEDURE

1 Group the students in fours and hand out a copy of the story to each group.

2 Ask the groups to flesh out the story by inventing extra biographical information about the characters and by adding extra details to the story. Each invention should be inserted in the appropriate place and written down in the margins of the photocopy. It should be in the style of the original. Allow 20 minutes.

3 Ask each group to pass their fleshed-out story to the next group, who then read it. Continue this process until each group has read all the fleshed-out stories.

VARIATION

This activity can work if you do not have access to a photocopier, but it takes a little longer. Here's how:

1 Ask each group to take a human interest story from your Story Bank (see page 28) and place (but not glue) it on a sheet of paper.

2 Proceed as in Stage 2 above.

3 Each group exchanges their story with another group. The groups now flesh out these second stories.

4 Bring each pair of groups together to share their work.

COMMENTS

There is much more to this activity than meets the eye. As each group adds to a story, they must ensure that content and style match the original. This leads to a lot of discussion and to discriminating writing.

3.20 Skeleton stories

LEVEL Intermediate and above

TIME 20–25 minutes

MATERIALS One short, human interest story

SKILLS Working from outline to text

ACTIVITY Familiarization with newspaper content

PREPARATION Select a short, human interest story such as the following:

Bottom-pincher owned up after wrong man held

Fashion designer Angela Holmes complained after a builder pinched her bottom in a crowded basement bar near York Minster but police arrested the wrong man, said Miss Colette Durkin, prosecuting, at York yesterday.

When Christopher Paul Kaye, 41, of Lawrence Street, York, learned of the error, he went to the police station.

Yesterday he was fined £80 after admitting indecent assault.

Mr John Howard, defending, said Kaye was enjoying a Christmas drink with friends when he jokingly pinched Miss Holmes's bottom. No evidence was offered against Stuart David Potter, of Park Grove, York, on a similar charge.

---

and write on the board only the basic information in your story. For example:

This is a story about Angela Holmes, a fashion designer, Christopher Paul Kaye, a builder, Miss Colette Durkin, a lawyer, and Stuart David Potter. It contains the words 'bottom' and 'wine bar'.

PROCEDURE 1 Pair the students and ask them to decide what the story is about.

2 Ask pairs to share their ideas. Then read the original story aloud.

VARIATION Distribute newspapers and ask each pair to find a story they think would work well for this activity. Each pair should cut out their story and write down the basic information in it. The basic information can then be exchanged with another pair's and the students either do the activity in class or for homework.

3.21 Completing a story

LEVEL	**Intermediate and above**
TIME	**45 minutes**
MATERIALS	**One story, access to a photocopier; for Variation 1, one story for every three students**
SKILLS	**Imaginative writing, evaluative reading, discussion of texts**
ACTIVITY	**Discovering how the sensational and the down-to-earth are combined in newspaper stories**
PREPARATION	**1** It is very important to find the right story for this activity. You are looking for a story in which the first, one of the middle, and the last paragraph will each stir the imagination when read by itself. This is the sort of text that works well for this activity, with the three suggested paragraphs highlighted:

Skyway robber steals half a million

By Tim Witcher in Paris

MORE THAN half a million pounds in cash has vanished in mid-air from the hold of an aircraft in a case that is baffling French detectives.

The money, collected from Corsican banks and post offices by a security company, was in a sack on an Air Inter flight from Bastia to Paris.

But when it reached the company's Paris headquarters the sack was found to contain nothing but old news-papers.

One theory is that the thief, possibly a woman, hid in a trunk in the hold and made the switch as the aircraft cruised at 30,000 ft and the security guards relaxed in the passenger cabin. The hold was pressurised, so the thief would have come to no harm at that altitude.

At Paris-Orly airport the guards signed for the sack as "OK". They noticed the lead seal was broken, but since this was a common occurrence dismissed its importance. "The guards thought it must have taken a knock in flight, as has happened in the past," a spokesman said.

One of the many Paris detectives investigating the theft yesterday said: "It is brilliant and, as far as we know, the first of its kind."

The security firm is used to the attentions of the French underworld, which has used machine-guns and even bazookas to hold up their vans. But mid-air robbery was a new departure.

Security guards had searched the hold of the aircraft on the tarmac at Bastia and were satisfied that the money was safe.

The broken seals and the presence on the flight of the trunk, weighing more than 150lbs, eventually led police to the "skyway robbery" theory.

The trunk, it was later discovered, was collected normally. "Ironically", said the detective, "they had to pay for some excess weight at the Paris freight terminal—probably the weight of 5.7 million francs in cash."

The surcharge was paid in cash so the robbers could not be traced and the address given for the trunk in case of loss or damage turned out to be false.

Police said it must have been a small man or a woman in the trunk, which was barely 5ft 6in long.

"We have learned another lesson," was all the security firm spokesman would say about the affair.

2 When you have found the ideal story, glue the first paragraph to the top of a sheet of paper, the middle paragraph to the middle of a second sheet, and the third paragraph to the bottom of a third sheet.

3 Make equal numbers of copies of each of the three sheets, but only enough for each student to get one of the sheets.

PROCEDURE

1 The students may work individually or in pairs. Give out one sheet to each individual or pair. Ask them to imagine the rest of the story and use the sheet of paper to complete it. Allow 20 minutes.

2 Display all the finished stories on the wall with those with the original first paragraph at the beginning and those with the original last paragraph at the end. Last of all, display the original story. Allow reading time and encourage small group discussion as the students are reading.

3 You can also build a task into the reading phase. For example, you could ask the students to make a list of stories that are close to the original, or of stories that are more interesting than the original.

VARIATION 1

If you do not have access to a photocopier, the activity will work provided that you have one story for every three students. This means that you have to find additional suitable stories.

VARIATION 2

Another interesting completion activity is to cut a story vertically two-thirds of the way through a column and ask the students to rewrite it. If you do this, it is important to make sure that the students do not attempt the virtually impossible task of reconstructing the original. You can avoid this by making it clear that they should imagine that they are journalists and the text represents snatches of a conversation they overheard which they want to turn into a story for their own newspaper. Remember that the longer the story, the easier this activity becomes. You can also divide the class and give half the students two-thirds of the story from the left-hand margin and the other half two-thirds from the right-hand margin.

COMMENTS

The idea of completing stories is obviously not a new idea. If you give parts of the class slightly different completion tasks related to the same text, it makes the activity much more interesting and stimulates the sort of reading follow-up suggested here. It also works particularly well for newspapers because you can choose a short, original, authentic piece of writing with which the students can compare their work.

3.22 Combining stories

LEVEL

Intermediate and above

TIME

Up to 60 minutes

MATERIALS

Story Bank (see page 28), access to a photocopier

SKILLS

Incorporating source materials in one's writing

ACTIVITY

Exploring possible human interest story subject-matter

PREPARATION

1 Choose one different human interest story from your Story Bank for every two students.

2 Make enough copies of another human interest story for every two students to have one. Each pair thus has two stories, one of which everyone else has, and one which only they have.

PROCEDURE

1 Pair the students and distribute the different human interest stories (see Preparation, stage 1) and the common story (see Preparation, stage 2) to each pair. Allow 40 minutes for each pair to write a single story which combines the two stories in front of them.

2 Ask the pairs to leave their two original stories and their combined story on their desks. Allow 20 minutes for the students to circulate reading each others' work.

VARIATION

The only way to get round the lack of a photocopier in this activity is to use a story from a coursebook as the common story which each pair combines with their own different stories chosen from your Story Bank.

COMMENTS

This activity is a variation on the well-known idea of combining two different stories to make a single composite one. What makes this variation more interesting is that at the reading stage the students recognize that they were all working with common material which each pair will have had to use very differently.

4 Working with pictures

It is worth considering whether a newspaper picture illustrates a story (the conventional view) or whether a story in fact supports a picture (as viewers of television news might think sometimes). In Britain, newsvendors' posters often promise the reader a picture, as though the picture is more important than the text. It is probably safe to assume that we look at the picture before (as well as after, sometimes) reading the text. It would be a rash person who claimed that descriptions in words are studied before the visual image.

The purpose of this argument is to remind ourselves that pictures do not merely supplement words, although as highly literate language teachers we may sometimes think of them in this way. The activities in this chapter treat texts and pictures as complementary and in a parallel relationship. This means that most are matching activities of one kind or another.

There are a number of practical points to bear in mind in this chapter:

1 Matching pictures and texts inevitably means cutting up newspapers, but usually you do not need current or even whole newspapers for this—the left-over pages from previous classes will do fine. So when the Materials heading lists newspapers, you can usually manage with left-overs.

2 Many picture-based activities are suitable for Elementary as well as Intermediate and Advanced students. This chapter is therefore more accessible to Elementary and Upper-elementary students than the other chapters.

3 If a student works with a picture, there is a natural tendency to think about it in the mother tongue. In several of these activities, you can encourage your students to think silently about a picture in English. This is discussed in more detail in the Comments on 4.13, 'My picture'.

The first activity in the chapter draws attention to the extent to which the categories 'text' and 'picture' do not account for the entire contents of newspapers. The last three activities (4.13–4.15) have an affective dimension. Activities 4.2–4.5 focus on what is illustrated by pictures, and activities 4.6–4.12 on how story and picture are related.

4.1 What is a picture?

LEVEL	**Elementary and above**
TIME	**25–30 minutes**
MATERIALS	**One newspaper for every two students**
SKILLS	**Scanning**
ACTIVITY	**Identifying what is neither text nor picture**

PROCEDURE

1 Ask the students to work in pairs, and distribute one newspaper to each pair.

2 The students should circle everything they find that is not either text or a photograph. This may include line drawings, lists, forms to complete, ruled lines, cartoons, crosswords, diagrams, logos, motifs, maps, charts, tables, etc. But do not tell the students what to look for in advance.

3 Bring pairs together to exchange newspapers and compare what they have found.

VARIATION

Once these features have been identified, can the students give each a name? Are they each separate features in their own right, or are there two or three categories within which they can be grouped?

COMMENTS

This is a very revealing activity which sensitizes the students to just how much you can find in newspapers that does not fall readily into the two stereotypical categories of text and picture, and to where in a newspaper it tends to occur.

4.2 Picture categories

LEVEL	**Elementary and above**
TIME	**30–40 minutes**
MATERIALS	**One newspaper for every four students**
SKILLS	**Devising broad categories**
ACTIVITY	**Recognizing what is most commonly illustrated**

PROCEDURE

1 Ask the students to work in fours and to spend 10 minutes deciding on the three categories (such as 'people', 'landscape',

etc.) they think will be sufficient to include every picture and illustration (including advertisements) that are found in newspapers.

2 Distribute a newspaper to each group and ask them to check the pictures against their categories. The three categories should be revised so as to accommodate as many of the pictures and illustrations as possible.

3 Allow time for inter-group discussion.

COMMENTS

This is a very revealing activity which raises our awareness of what we are shown in the newspapers.

4.3 Mood pictures

LEVEL

Elementary and intermediate

TIME

40 minutes

MATERIALS

One newspaper for every four students

SKILLS

Matching language and picture

ACTIVITY

Discovering the dominant themes in newspaper pictures

PROCEDURE

1 Ask the students to work in groups of four. Each group should decide on an adjective that could describe a newspaper photograph. Possible examples include 'aggressive', 'amorous', 'funny', 'happy', 'lucky', 'sad', 'unpleasant'.

2 Give each group a newspaper. Ask the groups to cut out any pictures that match their adjective. They should also cut out the accompanying texts. As each group finishes with a newspaper, they exchange it with another group.

3 When the groups have six or seven pictures on a single theme, they exchange them with another group. Each group tries to guess the other group's theme.

VARIATION 1

A simpler version of this activity involves only finding pictures that match the adjective and not bothering with the text. Although simple, this is still a worthwhile activity that teaches the students a lot about newspaper pictures. You can also use your Picture Bank (see page 28) instead of newspapers.

VARIATION 2

If you are working with intermediate or advanced groups, you can use this activity if you add a formal task related to the texts that accompany the pictures, like deciding to what extent each story relates to the group's theme.

COMMENTS   Remember that every picture that your students reject is also teaching them something as they decide why it does not fit their adjective.

4.4 Appropriate pictures

LEVEL   Intermediate and above

TIME   30 minutes per story

MATERIALS   One newspaper for every five students

SKILLS   Identifying relevant illustrations

ACTIVITY   Raising awareness of what is included in and omitted from newspaper pictures

PROCEDURE   1 Ask the students to work in pairs and hand out newspapers. Each pair should find and cut out a story that interests them which is accompanied by a photograph.

2 Once each pair has their story, ask them to study it carefully and either draw or describe a picture that would be more suitable than the one that already accompanies it.

3 The results should be displayed on the wall. Allow 10 minutes' reading time.

4.5 Picture visualization

LEVEL   Elementary and above

TIME   5–10 minutes plus 15 minutes one hour later

MATERIALS   One picture for every student plus five more

SKILLS   Memorizing in the mother tongue, recalling in English

ACTIVITY   Studying the detailed composition of newspaper and magazine pictures

PREPARATION   Cut out or select from your Picture Bank (see page 28) five more pictures than there are students in the class. Choose detailed pictures, and especially ones whose detail becomes more apparent the longer one looks at them. Colour magazines are often a better source of this kind of picture than newspapers.

PROCEDURE

1 Ask each student to choose a picture, and return to their desks with it. When everyone is sitting down, ask for three minutes' complete silence in which the pictures are committed to memory. Advanced students will be able to do this in English, but for less advanced students the activity works better if they memorize the picture in their mother tongue. At the end of the three minutes, explain that the class will do something else and not work on the pictures till later.

2 Allow at least an hour of other activities before pairing students. Ask each pair to find a little bit of personal space somewhere in the room where they cannot see either of their pictures. Each person then describes their picture to their partner in English—it is best if they each work with their eyes shut.

3 The students should take their partner to see the picture they described. Those who heard the descriptions should say what surprises them when they see the pictures.

VARIATION 1

If you work in a context where it is possible for each student to take their chair to a wall, ask them to sit down and display their pictures at viewing height before the three minute silence. This allows a special atmosphere of concentration to develop.

VARIATION 2

At the preparatory stage, glue the picture to one side of a sheet of paper and the accompanying story to the other. After Stage 3 above, the students can try and guess what stories accompanied the pictures before turning over to read them.

COMMENTS

Usually a person can remember the detail of a picture committed to memory in this way for at least a week. So you can delay Stage 2 for several days if this fits your timetable better.

4.6 Finding stories for pictures

LEVEL

Intermediate and above

TIME

45 minutes

MATERIALS

One picture and one newspaper for every four students, or your Story Bank (see page 28)

SKILLS

Reading for theme and making connections

ACTIVITY

Discovering what can be illustrated in a newspaper story

PREPARATION

Choose a distinctive picture, if possible a colour picture, and display it on the board.

PROCEDURE

1 Pair the students and give out newspapers or make your Story Bank available. Each pair should try to find a story they can connect with the picture. When they find their story, they cut it out, glue it to a sheet of paper, and write down the nature of the connection on the sheet. Each story sheet should be displayed on the board alongside the picture.

2 The pairs can repeat Stage 1 until there is a substantial display of stories round the picture, which the class can then read.

3 (This stage is optional.) Ask the students to work in groups of five to six. Take down the stories and share them among the groups. Each group then orders the stories according to how well they fit the picture.

VARIATION

At Stage 1, omit the stage where the pairs write down the nature of the connection between the story and the picture. Once each pair has chosen a story, they exchange it with another pair who try to guess the connection. When this is correctly guessed, it can be written on the story, which is then displayed on the board.

4.7 Finding pictures for stories

LEVEL

Upper-elementary and above

TIME

30–35 minutes

MATERIALS

One human interest story, one newspaper for every five students, glue, access to a photocopier (optional)

SKILLS

Identifying the major theme in a text

ACTIVITY

Discovering which pictures can illustrate a particular story

PREPARATION

Choose a human interest story and display it on the board or OHP. With larger classes, it is a good idea to make copies for each student too.

PROCEDURE

1 Pair the students and give out newspapers. Each pair should try to find a picture they can connect with the story. When they find their picture, they cut it out, glue it to a sheet of paper, and write down the nature of the connection on the sheet. Each picture sheet should be displayed on the board alongside the story.

2 The pairs can repeat Stage 1 until there is a substantial display of pictures round the story, which the class can then study.

3 (This stage is optional.) Ask the students to work in groups of five to six. Take down the pictures and share them among the

groups. Each group then orders the pictures according to how well they fit the story.

VARIATION

At Stage 1, omit the step where the pairs write down the nature of the connection between the picture and the story. Once each pair has chosen a picture, they exchange it with another pair who try to guess the connection. When this is correctly guessed, it can be written on the picture, which is then displayed on the board.

4.8 Matching pictures and stories

LEVEL

Upper-elementary and above

TIME

30–40 minutes

MATERIALS

Ten illustrated stories, glue

SKILLS

Reading for meaning at various levels

ACTIVITY

Matching pictures and text

PREPARATION

1 Cut out ten stories with pictures. Separate the pictures and the stories and glue each to a separate piece of paper.

2 Number the pictures from 1 to 10 and letter the stories from A to J, but so that the pictures and stories are not numbered and lettered logically—i.e. if you label the first picture '1' do not label the first story 'A'. Remember to make a list of what numbers and letters go together.

3 Display the pictures on one wall of the classroom and the stories on another.

PROCEDURE

Ask the students to study the pictures and the stories and try to match them. Encourage the students to begin by reading all the stories. Once they have a provisional list, they should consult each other.

COMMENTS

1 Matching pictures and stories is not a new idea, but it works especially well for newspapers because some matches are much easier to make than others. This means that a variety of reading skills from skim reading to in-depth, analytical study reading are required, as are various levels of re-reading.

2 You can easily adjust this activity to the level of your learners. For example, if there is only one story and picture of each type (football, accident, etc.), upper-elementary students can manage the activity. At the opposite end of the scale, for truly advanced students, you can use several stories of the same type.

Modals!

4.9 Predicting headlines and stories

LEVEL   Upper-elementary and above

TIME   25–30 minutes per picture + preparation time

MATERIALS   Illustrated stories, glue

SKILLS   Writing story outlines

ACTIVITY   Learning how pictures enable understanding of a text

PREPARATION   This can be done by the students in class time or, if you prefer, by yourself before class. Select interesting pictures and glue each to a sheet of paper. The accompanying headline and story should be glued to the back of the sheet. For each 25 minutes of classwork, you will need half as many prepared sheets as there are students in the class.

PROCEDURE   1 Pair the students and give each pair one picture sheet. Tell the students to study only the pictures and under no circumstances to turn them over and read the headlines and stories.

2 Each pair should decide on a likely headline and write it down under the picture.

3 Each pair decides what they think the accompanying story will be about and writes a one- or two-sentence summary of it under the headline.

4 When this is done, the students turn their pictures over and read the real stories.

5 If you wish, display the sheets picture side up and allow the students to circulate looking at the suggested headlines and story outlines before turning over to read the real stories. Allow one minute's reading time for every story. This makes a nice end to a lesson.

4.10 Captions

LEVEL   Upper-elementary and above

TIME   45 minutes

MATERIALS   One newspaper photograph for each student, glue

SKILLS   Matching picture and language imaginatively

ACTIVITY   Understanding the properties of captions

PREPARATION

1 Cut out one photograph of a person for each student. The photographs can be any size from head only to full length, but each must have a caption. Glue each photograph without its caption to a sheet of paper. Write the name of the person and a one-line biography under the picture. For example, under the photograph of John Hill (see below) you might write, 'A rich businessman and the owner of the Europa Shopping Centre'.

2 Write all the captions on the board.

PROCEDURE

1 Ask the students to copy the captions down. They should check that they understand each caption with their neighbours, by using a dictionary, and, if necessary, by asking you.

2 Ask each student to choose a photograph.

3 The students circulate showing each other their photographs. Each time a student is shown a photograph, they write the caption they think is the right one under it. Make it clear that the same caption can be used more than once. Humour can also be encouraged. For example, a possible caption for a photograph of the Queen waving might be, 'It's goodbye'.

John Hill – a rich businessman and owner of the Europa Shopping Centre.

power bid
Delighted
furious
Dog lover
A signal of victory
a nice little earner
It's goodbye
boost to his status
a signal of victory
Power bid

4 When the students have a number of possible captions under their photographs, reveal the original pairings.

VARIATION

Display the photographs on the wall. Ask the students to circulate, writing an appropriate caption under each photograph.

4.11 Best picture, story, and headline

LEVEL

Intermediate and above

TIME

50–60 minutes

MATERIALS

One set of a single day's newspapers

SKILLS

Matching text, title, and illustration

ACTIVITY

Distinguishing the different qualities of different newspaper presentations

PROCEDURE

1 Ask the students to work in groups of six to eight.

2 Give out a single day's set of newspapers and ask each group to choose a news story that features in at least four different papers. Make sure that each group chooses a different story.

3 When a group has chosen a story, they should cut out each newspaper's version of it, including the headline and any pictures that go with it.

4 Each group now tries to compose the best possible version by combining the best story, picture, and headline. The new versions can be displayed on the wall.

COMMENTS

1 This activity is only possible where you have a set of a single day's newspapers, preferably that day's.

2 This is an exercise in discrimination. The students are empowered as a result of rejecting several potential texts in the foreign language and pictures that represent the foreign culture.

4.12 Picture awards

LEVEL

Upper-elementary and above

TIME

40–60 minutes

MATERIALS

A complete set of that day's newspapers if possible, otherwise one newspaper for every five students.

SKILLS

Assessing the relationship between text and illustration

ACTIVITY

Looking for quality and relevance in pictures

PROCEDURE

1 Ask the students to work in groups of five to six and give each group a newspaper. Explain that as a group finishes with a newspaper, it should be exchanged with another group so that the students see as many newspapers as possible.

2 Ask each group to make two awards, one for 'Best photograph', the other for 'The photograph that goes best with the story it accompanies'. Each award should be accompanied by a one-line citation explaining why that particular picture and picture-story combination have been chosen.

3 Each group should work with a single paper at a time and keep a record of any likely pictures so that they can ask for that paper back again later.

4 When all the groups have chosen their pictures, they should be cut out and displayed on the wall together with the citations. Allow 10 minutes' reading time.

4.13 My picture

LEVEL	**Elementary and above**
TIME	**30–40 minutes**
MATERIALS	**One picture for every three students**
SKILLS	**Decision making**
ACTIVITY	**Relating to pictures**

PREPARATION

Cut out one picture for every three students. They may be in colour or black and white. Glue each picture to a sheet of paper and number it. Display the pictures around the classroom.

PROCEDURE

1 Each student makes a list of all their classmates.

2 Ask the students to move around the classroom looking at the pictures. Each student should choose a picture they can associate with. They should not reveal their choice.

3 Ask the students to return to their desks and decide which picture each of their classmates has associated with. They should write the number of the picture beside each of the names on their list of classmates.

4 When everyone has done this, ask the students to take their lists and go to the picture they associated with. They will now be able to see how many of their classmates they correctly associated with the right picture. Since you started with three times as many students as pictures, you would expect each student to have correctly associated three classmates with the right pictures. If anyone has scored five or six, they have magical powers!

5 Allow the students who are grouped around each picture to share the reasons why they associated with it.

COMMENTS

1 Although this activity does not involve newspaper language, it does give students a close personal interest in pictures, which are a good place to begin reading a foreign language newspaper. For this reason, try to choose pictures which are typical of newspapers.

2 Until Stage 5, this activity requires no spoken English. The students are likely to go through all the internal thought processes in their native language(s) unless you ask them to try thinking and decision making in English. If you do this, it becomes a very motivating activity since the students are aware that they have completed an extensive internal thinking process in English. And since the language required is a very restricted set consisting of not much more than numbers, it is possible to think through the activity in English even at an Elementary level.

4.14 My picture and my story

LEVEL

Upper-elementary and above

MATERIALS

One illustrated story for every four students

SKILLS

Decision making

ACTIVITY

Discovering how reliable a guide a picture is to its accompanying story

PREPARATION

Cut out one picture for every four students. They may be colour or black and white. Glue each picture to a sheet of paper and number it. Glue the story that accompanied the picture to the reverse of the sheet. Display the sheets around the classroom, picture side facing outward.

PROCEDURE

1 Ask the students to move around the classroom looking at the pictures. Tell them that the story accompanying each picture is glued to the back of the picture. Ask them to decide which story they want to read and then go to the appropriate picture.

2 When everyone has chosen their picture, the students grouped around each picture should share their reasons for choosing it before they take it off the wall and read the story together.

3 Each group should decide whether they are pleased, surprised, excited, amused, disappointed, or whatever by their story, and share their reactions with the other groups.

COMMENTS

Tell the students to try and think in English when they are deciding which story to read at Stage 1.

4.15 The good, the bad, and the ugly

LEVEL   **All levels**

TIME   **20–25 minutes.**

MATERIALS   **A set of pictures or your Picture Bank (see page 28)**

ACTIVITY   **Making aesthetic judgements about newspaper pictures**

PROCEDURE   1 Hand out newspapers or make your Picture Bank available. Ask the students to cut out all the beautiful and all the ugly pictures they can find.

2 When there are 15 or 20 of each, divide the students into two groups, one to work on the beautiful and one on the ugly pictures. Ask each group to order their pictures from most to least beautiful/ugly.

VARIATION 1   A more sophisticated variation involves gluing the picture to one side of a piece of paper and the accompanying story to the other. Then the groups can report back on the ugliest/most beautiful, explaining how they relate to their stories.

COMMENTS   1 This is a good activity for the start of the day, especially for those classes where some students tend to arrive late.

2 Although not an activity that is especially dependent on newspapers, it does give real insights into one dimension of newspaper pictures.

5 Project work

The activities in this chapter have one thing in common: none can be completed in a single lesson. They range from those that require half a day's work to those which are genuinely ongoing over several days or even, sometimes, weeks. This latter category often need to be fed with a regular supply of current newspapers, and are therefore easiest in an English-speaking context. Where this is the case, it is indicated under the heading 'Context'.

Sometimes a project can also be used to bridge the gap between in-class and out-of-class reading. If your students have out-of-class access to English-language newspapers, they may be encouraged to bring articles to class that they come across in their more extensive out-of-class reading. The projects that lend themselves most readily to out-of-class reading are 5.3, 5.7, 5.9, 5.10, 5.11, 5.12, 5.13, and 5.14.

5.1 From news to news story

LEVEL	**Intermediate and above**
TIME	**Half-day project**
MATERIALS	**Different photographs from a single story featured in several newspapers**
ACTIVITY	**Writing and laying out articles**
PREPARATION	Look for a story that is widely covered in the newspapers and accompanied by lots of photographs. When you find your story, cut out all the photographs from every newspaper and summarize the story in a single, full sentence. For example:

The IRA burst into a house in Londonderry and held a woman and three children at gunpoint while her husband was forced to drive a car bomb to an army checkpoint where it exploded, killing him and three soldiers.

Write this summary sentence on the board.

PROCEDURE

Ask the class to work in groups of four or five. Explain that each group should write a 300–500 word account of the story. This should be properly set out, with a headline and sub-headings, and be accompanied by photographs, which can be chosen from your collection. The groups should pay particular attention to the layout, including the relationship of photographs and text, and the number of columns to spread the story over. They may add any appropriate additional details that they would expect to find in the story.

Completed stories should be displayed on the wall alongside the original newspaper versions.

COMMENTS

This activity makes the students think hard about the relationship of text, headings, and photographs, and about the aesthetics of the layout.

5.2 Being a journalist

LEVEL

Intermediate and above

TIME

Half-day project

MATERIALS

Newspaper stories and features (see Preparation), audio or video recording (optional)

ACTIVITY

Acting as a journalist

PREPARATION

You will need to do a lot of preparation for this project. The students are going to act as journalists writing stories for you, the Editor. This means that you will have to prepare approximately two tasks per student. It often works well if tasks are related to an existing story or feature which you glue to an instruction sheet. Here are some ideas for instruction sheets:

- Choose a story from a popular paper, and under it write, 'Rewrite this story for our more educated readers.' (You can also do this the the other way round, i.e. rewriting a story from a quality newspaper for a less educated readership.)
- Cut out the first half of a feature article and under it write, 'The writer got half way through this feature when she was called away. Complete it for her, please.'
- 'I understand our rivals have a "Prime Minister goes shopping" story. No further information—invent one for us.'
- Cut out the page 1 lead story, and under it write, 'Write a comment column on this news story.'
- 'Write a "Sports Editor's Advice" column for the national football team.'

- Cut out a story with human interest potential and under it write, 'This story seems a bit thin—invent some human interest, please.'
- Make specific suggestions for ways in which a story could be expanded. For example:

Return by ear mail!

A YOUTH who had an ear bitten off in a brawl received it back through his letterbox — complete with earring —magistrates at Grantham, Lincs. heard yesterday.

Franz Smith, 19, his ear still bandaged, was bound over to keep the peace.

I like it, but can't you add something more? What does his girlfriend think? Who found it — his Mum? Health Risks? That sort of thing — whatever you like!

- Make available an audio or video recording of a single television or radio news item from that day with the following instuction: 'Listen to/watch this tape and write an entertaining version of it for the paper.'

PROCEDURE

1 Allow the students to choose whether to work individually, in pairs, or in small groups.

2 Place all the instruction sheets face down on the table and ask each student/pair/group to choose one. If they feel they cannot work with their chosen sheet, they should take another.

3 Your role is that of the Editor who may be consulted at any stage and who decides whether to accept a finished piece of work or send it back for revision. When a task is completed successfully, it should be displayed on the wall.

VARIATION

You can also impose time limits by suggesting that deadlines for copy are only 10 minutes away. This may help to make the task more realistic and pressures the students into rapid decision making and writing.

COMMENTS

1 You will find that students try to identify and then imitate the in-house style of the English-language newspaper they are familiar

with. This project therefore gives them an insight into the typical features and styles of English-language newspapers because they have had to think so carefully about them.

2 As soon as you open a newspaper, you will find lots of stories that lend themselves to this kind of treatment. You will be surprised how easily the ideas come when you have real newspapers to work with in front of you. And if you ask colleagues to help you after school or on a training day, it makes a very good in-service teacher development session—and provides you and your colleagues with lots of usable ideas.

5.3 Readers' competitions

LEVEL

Upper-intermediate and above

TIME

Half-day project

MATERIALS

Several newspapers and magazines

ACTIVITY

Designing a competition

PROCEDURE

1 Make newspapers and magazines available and ask the students to cut out all the competitions they can find, from crosswords and spot-the-ball to winning holidays and the chance to meet a famous person. These should be displayed on the walls and studied carefully.

2 Ask the students to work in groups of three to five to design a readers' competition. This will involve:

– deciding what sort of a competition it is to be;
– deciding on an appropriate prize;
– devising the competition itself: the final product should be typed up wherever possible and include any necessary artwork.

COMMENTS

1 If you ask the students to type their competitions, this may have to be done outside the half-day class time.

2 There are many newspaper features, such as competitions, that are often overlooked and yet which give a clear picture of the culture and its values. Other 'forgotten' areas include advertising, travel features, the financial pages, and announcements. At the same time as gaining insights into the culture of the relevant English-speaking society, this project encourages students to read carefully and for complete understanding and gives them an opportunity to be creative and original. Because competition design is difficult to take totally seriously, the students are also encouraged to think about the way they need to write down to an audience they must suppose to be less educated than themselves.

5.4 Radio reviews

LEVEL

Upper-intermediate and above

TIME

Half-day project

MATERIALS

Recording of a radio review, a complete set of newspapers for that day

ACTIVITY

Assessing and predicting which stories will be included in a radio review of papers; which stories are considered important by which papers

CONTEXT

Only possible where these materials are available

In many English-speaking countries, there are radio reviews of the national newspapers. In Britain, for example, a review of the national dailies is broadcast on BBC Radio 4 at 6.05, 6.40, and 7.40 every morning. Interestingly, it is very rare even for two of these three reviews to be identical.

This is a project which takes at least half a day and is only possible in countries where there is an English-language radio or television review of the daily papers (but see Variation). It must be done on the day the papers are published. It works better with advanced than with intermediate students. It makes an interesting half-day project on a summer course held in an English-speaking country. It focuses strongly on listening and reading, and gives interesting insights into the target culture. For this reason, it also works well as a half-day project on pre-sessional English for Academic Purposes courses where part of the focus is on socialization and where you want to encourage listening to the radio and reading newspapers.

PREPARATION

1 You will need to be up early to record the newspaper reviews—try to record as many of them as you can. This enables you to choose the most interesting version or the one with the widest cover.

2 You will also need a complete set of national daily newspapers. If you have more than 15 students in your class, two sets make things much easier.

3 You will also save 15 minutes of class time if you prepare a grid as overleaf and make two copies for each student.

PROCEDURE

1 It is best if the students work in groups of four or five. Explain that there is a radio review of the national daily papers each morning. Describe its typical characteristics—in Britain it usually covers four or five serious stories and one less serious story, lasts three to four minutes, and mentions at least two-thirds of the papers.

2 Each group should select the five or six stories they think will have been mentioned in that morning's review. This means they will have to scan all the papers in order to decide on the relevant stories. Allow about 45 minutes.

3 Now that each group has decided which stories will be in their version of the review, they must decide which newspaper(s) will be mentioned in relation to each story. This means that each group will need to find all the different versions of each story before they reach their decision. Allow one hour.

4 Ask each student to take a grid and complete it with the list of all the papers that their group expects to hear mentioned on the horizontal axis, and all the stories on the vertical axis. For the British press, the grid might look something like this:

	Europe & The Middle East crisis	Death of IRA Gunman	Prime Minister to visit Africa	State of the Economy	The Dog who talks			
The Independent	X							
Daily Telegraph	X							
Daily Express		X		X				
The Sun		X		X				
The Star		X						
The Times		X						
Daily Mail			X					
Daily Mirror				X	X			
The Guardian				X				

The boxes that are ticked indicate the papers which will be mentioned in relation to each story.

Allow 15 minutes if you have already prepared and photocopied the matrix, and 30 minutes if you have to draw a specimen on the board for each student to copy down twice (once for this stage, once for the next stage).

5 Listening.
In Britain, the radio review is typically spoken very fast indeed, so you will need to break the listening task down into separate steps:

(a) Listen only for the names of the newspapers, which should be entered on the horizontal axis of the second copy of the grid in the order mentioned. (You will probably have to play the tape twice, even for this exercise.)

(b) Listen again, but do not write. This time each group tries to decide how many stories are being reviewed and what their themes are. These should then be entered on the vertical axis.

(c) Listen for stories and papers linked together and tick the appropriate boxes. You may have to play the tape twice and allow discussion within each group between the two playings.

6 Each group should compare their prediction with the actual review. How successfully did they predict what would be in it?

7 Allow the students to get together with classmates who were working in other groups so that the different groups' predictions can be compared.

8 Allow each group time to compare the newspapers with what they heard in the review—can they find any of the stories? Can they underline or highlight any actual sentences which were quoted in the review?

9 Tell the class the time(s) when the newspaper review is on the radio and at what frequency it is broadcast. Encourage the students to listen to the review each day and, on the basis of what they hear, go out and buy themselves the paper of their choice. They should try and track down one of the stories they heard mentioned in the review.

VARIATION

For non-English-speaking environments

1 Prepare for the project by recording the BBC World Service news.

2 Take the local English-language newspaper(s) and any other English-language newspapers you can get hold of for the same day and the next day to class.

3 Ask the students to work in groups of four or five. Each group should select seven or eight stories which they think will be mentioned on the World Service news. They should decide what

order the stories will be mentioned in and which main points will be picked out.

4 Ask the groups to write their seven or eight chosen stories in the spaces along the top of the matrix, i.e. on the vertical axis.

5 At the listening stage, the students enter the actual stories on the horizontal axis of the matrix and tick the boxes where their predictions were fulfilled.

6 Follow Stages 6, 7, and 8 of the activity.

7 Discuss the differences between the World Service news and the newspaper coverage. This may well lead to discussing perspective, bias, and even censorship.

8 Tell the class the times when the World Service news is on air and the frequencies at which it is broadcast. Encourage the students to listen each day and compare this version of the news with the news presented in the local English-language and mother-tongue newspapers.

5.5 Papers from the past

LEVEL	**Intermediate and above**
TIME	**Half-day project**
MATERIALS	**Three or four newspaper cuttings**
ACTIVITY	**Reconstructing the past**

PREPARATION

Take a sheet of newspaper and expose it to sunlight for two or three weeks and it will fade and look as though it might be a hundred years old.

Take an old suitcase and fill it with five or six small objects, articles of clothing, and keepsakes from a byegone age, a couple of old photographs, and three or four appropriately chosen faded newspaper cuttings (see Comments), and you have got a magic box around which the class can imagine a fantasy world.

PROCEDURE

It is usually better to divide the class into groups of six to eight for this project. Display the contents of the suitcase and ask each group to come up and look at them carefully. Once they have done this, each group should spend some time trying to make up a story that relates all the objects and newspaper cuttings. Try to set this up in such a way as to give the students the sense that what they are doing is reconstructing a real past world rather than merely inventing a story. Once a group has made up their story, they can do a number of things:

- work on an improvisation of part of the story that they have invented;
- contribute something written of their own to the suitcase—a letter to future generations or an account of the mystery they think they have solved;
- write a further article that might have been found in the suitcase but was not;
- record a radio broadcast around the contents of the suitcase.

At the end of the session, each group shares their work with the class.

COMMENTS

1 Good sources of suitable newspaper cuttings to put in the suitcase are:

- local newspapers, particularly the not very interesting family and petty crime stories you can find in them;
- letters to newspapers;
- feature articles about unknown people (but remove any dates or time references);
- genuine old newspapers (we found lots under the carpets when we moved house);
- births, marriages, and deaths columns;
- *Chronicle of the Twentieth Century* (Random Century, new edition 1992).

2 Newspapers have a vital role to play in this activity because they contribute a sense of reality. Whatever the students do with the materials, they must respect the facts contained in the newspaper cuttings and build everything they create around them.

Acknowledgement
I learned the 'magic suitcase' idea from Phil Byrne.

5.6 Surveys

LEVEL   **Intermediate and above**

TIME   **Whole day or three sessions (see Guidelines: 1, below)**

MATERIALS   **One newspaper article**

ACTIVITY   **Conducting a survey to examine the assumptions made in newspapers**

BACKGROUND   In *Inside Meaning* (Swan 1975), there is a newspaper article which claims that visitors to the Shakespeare theatre at Stratford-upon-Avon spend money only in the theatre and not in the town too.

For this reason, they are said to be a less desirable kind of tourist than non-theatre-goers. When we first came across this story, we decided to test its accuracy. Accordingly, we designed an elaborate questionnaire, and all the students went out in search of people who would admit to having been to Stratford in the last twelve months to ask them questions about what they had done there and how much money they had spent. As the students began to return and compute their findings, we soon realized that we were going to be able to decide the merits of the case on the basis of real evidence. The last pair of students returned in triumph half an hour after the agreed time: they had met a tour guide who had taken a coachful of fifty tourists to Stratford, and from whom they had found out all there was to know. Nevertheless, our basic idea was a good one, and we have often done survey work since.

The Stratford article is by no means an isolated one. Newspapers frequently make claims about people's attitudes, interests, beliefs, and habits which your students can test in a survey. Sometimes these are based on 'research', sometimes they are just the assumptions of journalists. It is worth collecting articles of this kind when you spot them, since a survey based on newspaper materials is only possible when you have the right article to start with.

GUIDELINES

There are a number of basic rules to keep in mind:

1 You must have a clear idea of how much time you can afford to spend on each stage:

- The class will need to read and understand the original article and design the Questionnaire (up to two hours).
- The students will need to conduct the survey (up to one hour in winter, maybe longer in summer).
- The class will need time to collect all the findings and decide how to display them: which groups/pairs will summarize which parts of the Questionnaire and what sort of graphs, bar charts, pie charts, or other appropriate figures will they make?
- You may be able to put aside a whole day for a survey project, but you will probably need three sessions on three separate days.

2 Students often need to be given confidence before they go into the street to ask strangers a set of questions. It is a good idea to rehearse the initial approach, which will include an explanation that the survey is part of an English language learning activity.

3 Even in a non-English-speaking country, it is usually possible to find sufficient people who understand English for survey work in English to be possible.

4 We have found it works well to get students to interview in pairs in the street and individually if they stay in the School or College buildings.

5 There are particular moments at which surveys work especially well:

- If an election is called and the newspapers suggest that most people favour this or that person or party;
- In January, when the newspapers are full of predictions for the New Year—do most people agree with them or not?
- If there is an international crisis and the newspapers claim that most people favour a particular course of action;
- When statistics about lifestyle are released.

People often want to give you their views or information about themselves at such moments. We have known students come back into the classroom in ecstatic mood after conducting a survey and tell us that they have never spoken to so many native speakers in so short a time.

Newspaper article
Here is a newspaper article which would lend itself to survey work, certainly in Britain and perhaps, if adapted appropriately, in other countries too:

Britons 'put higher value on leisure than work'

By Richard Evans
Media Editor

A HIGHER proportion of people in Britain place less value on work than any other country in Western Europe, according to a survey released yesterday.

The survey, based on interviews conducted by the European Value Systems Study Group, found that 12 per cent of the British consider work of little importance, compared to an average of 4.5 per cent for Europe as a whole.

Britons also believe, along with people in Scandinavia, the Netherlands and Germany, that leisure is more important than work.

However, at the same time, most people in Britain—83 per cent—said that they took a great pride in their work, compared to a western European average of 40 per cent.

An "interesting job" (72 per cent) followed by "good pay" (68.5 per cent) were regarded as the most important aspects in Britain, whereas the European average favoured good pay (69 per cent) and "pleasant work colleagues" (65 per cent).

The survey also found that British citizens trust the trade unions and major companies less than the European average (which is already low), and have even less confidence in the social security system. Throughout Western Europe, family, friends, work and leisure were all rated as "very important" or "quite important", with religion and politics rated a great deal lower.

These are among the early findings of the survey, released at a conference in Liverpool on Roman Catholic social teaching. Changes in working practices and the challenge posed by unemployment were among the main themes of the four-day conference, which ends tomorrow.

5.7 Topics in the news

LEVEL	**Upper-intermediate and above**
TIME	**One hour per day over a week to ten days**
MATERIALS	**Consecutive days' newspapers**
ACTIVITY	**Following ongoing themes**
CONTEXT	**Only possible where enough newspapers are available**

Sometimes the newspapers spend several days on a particular topic, for example:

- the weather (when it is hotter or colder than usual);
- festivals (for example, Christmas or the New Year);
- a new fashion or invention;
- the state of education or of marriage in society;
- medical matters;
- a dramatic trial or court case;
- a celebrity in the news.

When the papers are in one of these moods, it is a good time for the class to mount a display of the various treatments of the chosen topic. Put aside an hour a day for collecting, displaying, and discussing articles on your theme. As the days pass, it becomes easier to trace the development of the story and to try and predict how it will continue and even, perhaps, conclude.

VARIATION   **for Business English**

This project works particularly well for Business English students who can follow an ongoing financial story such as a take-over, currency crisis, company in the news, privatization, Government intervention in business, or fiscal or monetary policy. It is also in the nature of business stories that they are not one-day wonders and for that reason it is easier to run this project at virtually any time with Business English students.

COMMENTS   This project is only possible if you have an ample supply of current newspapers. Its rationale lies in its topicality, which provides an opportunity for students to study the relationship between an environmental phenomenon and the newspapers' view of it. It is therefore an ideal project for an ESL class.

5.8 Class newspapers

LEVEL   **Intermediate and above**

TIME   **Occasional project**

ACTIVITY   **Making a newspaper**

The idea of a class newspaper is an old one. Here are a number of slightly lateral thoughts that may help you make creating a class newspaper more interesting (they are not all compatible with one another):

1 Each student becomes a reporter and tries to ferret out something unusual.

2 The paper contains only stories about members of the class. All the stories should be newsworthy and previously unknown to fellow students.

3 Stories that refer to members of the class should contain pseudonyms rather than real names—this adds spice to reading the paper.

4 The newspaper should be set in the future—in the year 2100, or when everyone is 10 or 20 or 30 years older, for example.

5 The paper should be modelled page for page on the structure of a real newspaper and displayed on the wall as it is being put together alongside the model.

6 The paper should be a compendium of the most remarkable things the students have done.

7 Each student should be responsible for obtaining one guest contribution from someone not in their class.

5.9 Collages

LEVEL   **Intermediate and above**

TIME   **Occasional or ongoing project**

MATERIALS   **Supply of newspapers**

ACTIVITY   **Choosing and arranging articles to fit a theme**

Collage making lends itself well to project work because a collage need never be complete—there is always a place to add in something new. Students often enjoy collage work because they feel it to be as much a challenge to their artistic judgement as a test of language skills. Sometimes a collage can be completed in half a day, sometimes it may be an ongoing piece of work. Some collages are essentially individual, others may be whole class projects. All are a form of display. Here are some suggestions for using newspaper materials in collage work:

1 Collages of similar items:

- the same type of story;
- on a common theme (for example, childhood, laughter, violence);
- sharing a common vocabulary;
- about a particular person.

2 Headline collages—run a headline strip all round the classroom with each new item connected in some (clever) way to its neighbour.

3 Collages as puzzles to be solved:

- with the name of the dominant person/people removed;
- ask fellow students to discover the right order in which to read the stories;
- with a hidden connection between each story or picture;
- as a charade: the articles and pictures in the collage give clues to the name of a famous person, film, book, etc.

4 Collages as visions of particular countries/societies.

5 Collages as presents (See 6.5, 'A collage for a friend').

6 Working from a teacher-prepared collage of, say, 'Life in Britain': how would the students want to change the society to make it acceptable to themselves? Which items would they retain in a collage of their own on the same theme and which pictures and stories would they add?

7 Collages built around a symbol—for instance, a dollar sign, a circle, or a gender symbol. Or collages arranged in the shape of a symbol. It is best to allow each student or group to choose their own symbol.

8 Collages stimulated by, or built up around, (a choice of) teacher-provided materials, such as: a proverb, a map, a picture, a quotation, a poem, the title of a book or film, or a word (hospital, prison, school, etc.).

9 Spoken or semi-improvised representations or performances of collages that are on display.

COMMENTS

Remember to allow the students as much freedom as possible in the choice of collage theme and the stories or pictures that illustrate it.

5.10 Awards

LEVEL	**Intermediate and above**
TIME	**Occasional or ongoing project**
MATERIALS	**A range of different newspapers**
ACTIVITY	**Looking for quality in newspapers**

The professional associations that represent the newspaper industry frequently give awards for best reporter, best news coverage, best feature writer, best photograph, best sports/arts/financial reporting, best newspaper, etc.

Giving newspapers awards makes a very nice project because it involves giving the students the power to make decisions. It is also convenient and flexible: for instance, one can spend a long lesson giving an award in some area and then not come back to the award theme for a week or two. This flexibility means that it can be a ongoing project which does not adversely affect the normal way one uses class time.

Suitable categories of award include: design and layout, tactful handling of tragic themes, comprehensive coverage, readability, awareness of minority readerships (children, foreign visitors, etc.) as well as the more expectable best political story, best human interest story, etc. Very often your students will come up with a whole series of award ideas and you can afford to let them choose which they want to work with.

Looking for quality in newspapers is a motivating and revealing activity in itself and one which non-native speakers very much enjoy.

Finally, where students have out-of-class access to English-language newspapers, they can be asked to keep an eye open for potential award-winning items on a fairly open-ended basis. This also motivates out-of-class reading.

5.11 Will it run?

LEVEL	**Intermediate and above**
TIME	**Daily for a week: Day 1—30 minutes; Subsequent days—20+ minutes**
MATERIALS	**Daily supply of current newspapers**
ACTIVITY	**Assessing and following ongoing stories**

CONTEXT	**Only possible where several English-language newspapers are available regularly**

PREPARATION Either buy a complete set of each day's papers to take to class, or ask each student to bring a specific newspaper.

PROCEDURE **Day 1** (Monday): Ask the students to work individually or in pairs or small groups, and give out newspapers. Each group selects (1) a story and (2) a picture of someone they expect to find in the papers each day for the rest of that week. These should be displayed on the wall.

Days 2–5 (Tuesday–Friday): The students comb the newspapers looking for stories/pictures on the same theme, which are then added to the wall display.

COMMENTS **1** Sometimes it works well to encourage learners to make different kinds of display. For example:
– linear: Monday→Friday;
– a spiral radiating outwards from Monday;
– a pattern tracing different threads, etc.

2 This project gives the students the important sense that each day's newspapers are members of a continuing series. It encourages the students to look forward to reading the next day's newspapers.

3 Discussion may ensue naturally from this activity.

5.12 People in the news

LEVEL **Intermediate and above**

TIME **Occasional or ongoing project: 20 minutes each day**

MATERIALS **At least one current newspaper each day**

ACTIVITY **Increasing background knowledge of people in the news**

This project works best where you see a class every day and have access to at least one English-language newspaper a day. One of its aims is to establish a familiarity with people in the news. This is important because knowing who is being written about makes the newspapers much more interesting. Once you have set the project up, you can spend 15–20 minutes on it at the beginning of each day.

PROCEDURE **1** Explain that the class is going to build up a large body of information about well-known people in the newspapers. The first task is to decide on the categories under which to list people. Get the class to make suggestions. You may decide to start with a limited number of categories, such as 'sport', 'entertainment', 'politics', or 'the rich and famous', and to have a miscellaneous category for people who do not fit into any of the given groups. After a week or two you can sort this 'miscellaneous' category out into two or three specific categories.

2 Once the categories have been decided on, ask each student to take a page of that day's newspaper and find a person in the news. Each student then takes a small piece of paper and in a single sentence writes down the name, occupation and current activities of their 'person in the news'. This should be dated. So a typical 'person in the news' sentence might look like this:

Paul Gascoigne, or 'Gazza', the famous English footballer, has been advised to train harder by his manager—15th December

3 While the students are finding their first set of 'people in the news', designate an area of classroom wall for each category and make a set of signs:

People in the news—Sport
People in the news—Politics
People in the news—Entertainment
People in the news—The rich and famous
People in the news—Miscellaneous.

4 Once each student has found their 'person in the news', they display their one-sentence biographies/story summaries under the appropriate sign and the class then circulates reading them.

5 Set aside a few minutes each day for students to find their 'people in the news'. Remember to allow more reading time as the walls get more crowded.

6 After 10–15 days, when the walls are becoming crowded, you can allocate a group of students to each category and ask them (1) to remove the names of people no longer in the news, or (2) to copy the names and biographies onto single sheets of paper. If you repeat (2) from time to time, it is a good idea to colour code the single sheets so that more recent 'people in the news' can be distinguished from less recent.

7 Remember to keep an eye on the 'miscellaneous' category to see whether it can be rationalized.

FOLLOW-UP

The purpose of the project is to make newspapers more readable by increasing the students' background knowledge about people in the news. Effective ways of encouraging this include:

1 Having sessions from time to time where the students look for references in that day's paper to people already on the walls.

2 Selecting one prominent 'person in the news' from each

category and cutting out stories about them each day for a week. Do they get a good or a bad press?

3 Selecting one prominent 'person in the news' from each category and looking for stories about them each day for a week with the intention of writing a substantial biography.

5.13 Winners and losers

LEVEL	**Elementary and above**
TIME	**30 minutes each day for a week**
MATERIALS	**Daily supply of current newspapers**
ACTIVITY	**Increasing familiarity with people in the news**
CONTEXT	**Only possible where a daily supply of newspapers is available**

PREPARATION

Either buy a set of each day's newspapers to take to class, or ask each student to buy a specific newspaper.

PROCEDURE

1 Divide the class into as many groups as you have different daily newspapers and give each group a front page. In a mixed-ability group, the more advanced groups get the 'quality' papers.

2 Each group writes down the name of every person on the front page and divides them into 'Winners' and 'Losers' on the basis of what is written about them.

3 Repeat Stage 2 every day for at least a week.

VARIATION

This also works well with long-running financial stories on Business English courses .

COMMENTS

This activity helps learners to break into the vicious circle: if you do not know who the papers are writing about you will not be motivated to read them; and if you are not motivated to read them, you will not know who they write about.

5.14 The picture gallery

LEVEL

Elementary to intermediate

TIME

Occasional or ongoing project: 20–25 minutes each day

MATERIALS

Daily supply of current newspapers

ACTIVITY

Looking at who appears most often in newspaper photographs

CONTEXT

Only possible where a daily supply of newspapers is available

PROCEDURE

Set aside 20–25 minutes each day for the class to mount a display of the most photographed people each day for a week. Make sure the captions (and, if you wish, the accompanying stories) are included in the display.

VARIATION 1

You can set aside extra time each Friday to turn the gallery into a display of the most photographed people each week.

VARIATION 2

If you have an extensive gallery collected over some time, you can re-organize the display, which will probably be set out on a day-by-day basis, in some new way. The possibilities include:

- according to the number of appearances people make;
- according to the roles a person is photographed in;
- by categories, such as politics, sport, entertainment, daily life;
- from the famous to the notorious.

6 Personal responses

This chapter contains 19 activities that bring together responses to newspaper materials and personal experiences, memories, and feelings. The rationale for this approach is that when we read, we only value as important what we absorb into the deeper level of our experience. Because the activities in this chapter give more prominence to the students' feelings, they are arguably less overtly instructive in relation to newspapers. They may compensate for this by playing a more important part in personal development.

Almost every activity in the chapter is about personal response to newspaper materials. Usually the students select the materials that evoke these responses themselves. The activities therefore often produce sets of newspaper stories and articles chosen by the students specifically for their effect. These materials should be added to your Story Bank (see page 28).

Person-centred education can be expected to value student choice and student response highly. The 19 activities in this chapter typically feature both in varying proportions. The first activity might almost have been found in Chapter 3 and the second in Chapter 2—these are bridge-building activities that link this chapter with the earlier ones. The next set of activities, 6.3–6.12, focus on choice, and the remaining activities, 16.3–6.19, on response, although as you will see when you look at the last few choice and the first few response activities, this distinction is not so absolute.

6.1 Your headlines, my stories

LEVEL	**Upper-elementary and above**
TIME	**15 minutes per story**
MATERIALS	**Very short, simple stories**
SKILLS	**Planning story outlines**
ACTIVITY	**Predicting newspaper story content**
PREPARATION	Choose two or three simple, very short stories with very distinctive headlines. ('Bottom pincher owned up after wrong man held' (see page 75) or 'Skyway robber steals half a million' (see page 76) would be perfect examples.)

PROCEDURE

1 Ask the students to work in groups of three.

2 Read the headline aloud and write it on the board. Allow three to five minutes' absolute silence while each student imagines the story that follows. They may make notes if they wish.

3 Allow up to 10 minutes while the groups compare their imagined versions and decide on the likeliest.

4 Read the original story aloud.

This procedure can be repeated with a second story.

VARIATION

Let each group choose their own headline and story. You can then use these in class. Remember to find an alternative activity for the group whose story you are using.

6.2 What's happening to people like me?

LEVEL

Intermediate and above

TIME

45 minutes

MATERIALS

One newspaper for every five students

SKILLS

Scanning, making lists, exchanging information

ACTIVITY

Discovering what makes people newsworthy

PROCEDURE

1 Ask each student to draw up a short, factual, background description of themselves that details age, sex, occupation, family status, and, if they wish, interests and character.

2 Give out newspapers and ask each student to find out what is happening to other people with the same or similar backgrounds. They should make a list of all the things all the other people of roughly the same age, sex, occupation, and family status are doing.

3 Ask the students to work in groups of four or five and exchange the information they have discovered.

COMMENTS

This activity works best in classes where students do not know each other well, where it can be used as an activity that helps the students to get to know more about each other. It also works well with groups who do know one another well, particularly if you ask the students to include interests in their background descriptions.

6.3 Which do you choose?

LEVEL   **Intermediate and above**

TIME   **Up to 60 minutes**

MATERIALS   **One newspaper for every six students, or your Story Bank (see page 28), glue**

SKILLS   **Reading for interest**

ACTIVITY   **Familiarization with the subject-matter of newspaper stories**

PROCEDURE   **1** Give out newspapers or make your Story Bank available. Ask each student to choose two stories which interest them and glue them to separate sheets of paper.

2 The idea is to offer fellow students a choice between these two stories. Each student will need to frame a one-sentence question along the lines of:

> Would you like to read a story about a woman who found a lot of money buried in her garden or a story about a man who fell out of a plane and survived?

> Would you prefer to read a story about an escaped prisoner or a story about new discoveries relating to the greenhouse effect?

3 The students should circulate asking each other the 'which do you choose' questions and writing the name of each fellow student under whichever story they choose.

4 When everyone has asked all their classmates their question, the stories should be displayed on the wall. Each student then reads only the stories they have chosen.

COMMENTS   **1** This is an easy way of creating a sense of reading for interest in the language classroom. And in the process the students learn a lot about the subject-matter of newspapers.

2 If you are giving out newspapers rather than using your Story Bank, the activity works best when each newspaper is for a different day.

6.4 A present from the Press

LEVEL	**Elementary and above**
TIME	**15–20 minutes**
MATERIALS	**One newspaper for every six students, small pieces of card**
SKILLS	**Selective, targeted reading**
ACTIVITY	**Exploring the extent to which newspaper materials are acceptable to others**

PROCEDURE

1 The students each write their names on small squares of card and then circulate for half a minute exchanging cards.

2 Stop the process and ask each student to find a 'present' (picture or story) for the person whose card they are holding. It should be picture or story that their classmate will be pleased with.

3 The picture or story should be cut out and given to the person named on the card together with a simple explanation of why it has been chosen.

4 As the students get their presents, they can show them to those of their classmates who have also received theirs.

VARIATION

Headline collages can also make acceptable presents (see activity 6.5).

COMMENTS

1 This activity makes a nice end to a session or a unit on newspapers, especially where there is a good rapport in a class.

2 If you do this activity a few times, you will find you remember the presents you gave and were given for a long time.

6.5 A collage for a friend

LEVEL	**Intermediate and above**
TIME	**45 or 60 minutes**
MATERIALS	**One newspaper for every five students**
SKILLS	**Reading for a purpose**
ACTIVITY	**Discriminating between newspaper stories**

PROCEDURE

1 Ask each student to think of someone they like who speaks more English than they do—this could be someone who speaks English as a second or foreign language, or a native speaker. (You may decide to rule yourself out, or you may decide to say nothing about whether you could be their chosen person.)

2 Give out newspapers and explain that they have 45 minutes (or 60 if you prefer) to find stories their friend would be interested in and make a collage out of them.

3 At the end of the lesson, encourage them (or even put aside time) to write a short letter to the friend explaining what happened in class and enclosing the collage as a present.

VARIATION

It is also possible to make collages for other purposes. For example, each student chooses a story that interests them and then looks for a suitable background of pictures and headline fragments amongst which to set it.

COMMENTS

This also makes a good homework or self-access task.

6.6 I chose this story because ...

LEVEL

Intermediate and above

TIME

40–45 minutes

MATERIALS

Stories, glue

SKILLS

Reading for meaning, justifying choice of story, discussing newspaper reading

ACTIVITY

Discovering what proportion of stories relate to the reader

PREPARATION

Choose one-and-a-half times as many stories as there are students in the class and glue each one to a large sheet of paper. Display these around the classroom.

PROCEDURE

1 Ask the students to circulate, reading the stories until they find one that attracts them.

2 When a student finds a story, they take it back to their desks and write under it:

I chose this story because ...
and because ...
It reminds me of ...

and complete each sentence with something true for themselves.

3 When they have done this, they replace the story on the wall and choose a second story.

4 Stop the activity after 25 minutes and allow 10–15 minutes' reading time. Encourage students who have chosen the same stories to discuss their choices.

COMMENTS

If you can get natural conversations springing up at Stage 4, this activity becomes an authentic replication of what we often do when we read newspapers in our own language.

6.7 That's nearly me

LEVEL

Upper-elementary and above

TIME

30–40 minutes

MATERIALS

One newspaper for every five students, or your Story Bank (see page 28)

SKILLS

Evaluative reading

ACTIVITY

Discovering the motives of people written about in the newspapers

PROCEDURE

1 Give out newspapers or make your Story Bank available. Ask each student to look for a story about someone who did more or less but not exactly what they would have done in the same circumstances. They should continue reading stories until they find the right person. Allow 15 minutes.

2 Ask the students to work in pairs or threes and explain which story they chose, who they would have acted like, and how they would have been just that little bit different.

COMMENTS

This activity works surprisingly well with political stories.

6.8 Who would I be?

LEVEL

Upper-elementary and above

TIME

40–45 minutes

MATERIALS

One page of human interest stories, access to a photocopier (but see Variation)

SKILLS

Reading and decision making, discussion

ACTIVITY

Associating one's own experience with that of the newsworthy

PREPARATION

Choose a page of human interest stories from the popular press. It is important that every story mentions at least two people. Make a copy of this page for each student—if necessary, copy it in two halves.

PROCEDURE

1 Give out a copy of the page to each student and ask them to read each story and decide which character in it acted most similarly to the way they would have done. Encourage them to think carefully and honestly about these decisions and, if they wish, make notes. Allow 20 minutes.

2 Ask the students to work in groups of four or five and share their decisions.

VARIATION

If you do not have access to a photocopier, you can still do this activity. Here's how:

1 Ask the students to work in groups of four or five and give each group a page of human interest stories. They should cut the separate stories out.

2 Each student takes and reads a story and makes their decision, as in Stage 1 in Procedure above.

3 Each student passes the story to the next person in the group, who reads it and makes their decision.

4 Continue this process until all the members of the group have read the stories (or until a certain period of time has passed, with large classes), after which they share their decisions.

6.9 Someone I'd change places with— well, nearly

LEVEL

Intermediate and above

TIME

30–40 minutes

MATERIALS

One newspaper for every five students, or your Story Bank (see page 28)

SKILLS

Discriminating reading, discussion

ACTIVITY

Relating to the newsworthy

PROCEDURE

1 Give out newspapers or make your Story Bank available, and ask each student to try and find someone in a story who they would genuinely change places with. Or if they cannot find anyone that they would actually change places with, at least someone who they would very much like to be. Allow 15–20 minutes.

2 Ask the students to work in threes and share the people they have chosen and the reasons for their decisions.

VARIATION

An interesting variation on this activity is to ask the students to try and find an ideal partner for themselves from amongst the people who feature in newspaper stories and photographs. Once each student has a partner, there are all sorts of fantasy activities one can do—writing to one's partner, recording a message for one's partner, meeting relatives with one's partner, wondering about the first meeting, hypothesizing one's partner's views of oneself, etc.

6.10 Sharing a chosen story

LEVEL

Upper-elementary and above

TIME

30 minutes

MATERIALS

One newspaper for every five students, or your Story Bank (see page 28)

SKILLS

Reading aloud, justifying choices, discussion

ACTIVITY

Presenting and discussing newspaper stories

PROCEDURE

1 Ask the students to work in groups of five or six. Give out newspapers or make your Story Bank available and ask each student to choose a story which interests them.

2 Allow five minutes for the students to prepare themselves (1) to read their story aloud to colleagues, and (2) to explain precisely why it interested them.

3 Ask the students to read their stories to the other members of their group and explain why they chose them. There should be a short discussion of each story after it has been read aloud.

VARIATION

Instead of asking the students to read the stories aloud, ask them to describe each one, along with their reasons for choosing it. When all the stories have been described, anyone in the group can ask to have a story read aloud.

COMMENTS

Because each student knows that their colleagues have taken the same trouble to choose a story as they have, they are strongly motivated to listen carefully to the reading and the explanation of why the story was chosen. The short discussion is an important natural final stage—it helps to integrate the skills rather than treating each as discrete.

6.11 Classifying stories

LEVEL

Intermediate and above

TIME

30 minutes

MATERIALS

One newspaper for every five students, or your Story Bank (see page 28), glue

SKILLS

Justifying a story category

ACTIVITY

Judging newspaper materials affectively

PROCEDURE

1 Give out newspapers or make your Story Bank available. Ask each student to find a story that interests them, cut it out, and classify it in one of three categories that relate to the emotions or feelings produced by the story. The teacher determines the categories—*blue*, *green*, and *red* work well. The story should be glued to a sheet of paper and an explanation supplied. For example:

This is a blue story because it's very sad.
or
This is a red story because it's about fire.

Other good categories include:

– *body, mind, soul*
– *earth, air, fire, water*
– *heaven, hell, purgatory*

2 Designate a wall for each category and have the students display the stories on the appropriate wall.

3 As the students finish, they should read the other stories that are going up.

COMMENTS

This is an excellent way of getting the class to select the stories that interest them and that you might want to work with later—a newspaper equivalent of Community Language Learning, in the sense that the students contribute the materials the class is going to work on.

6.12 Categories of story

LEVEL Intermediate and above

TIME 30–40 minutes

MATERIALS One newspaper for every five students, or your **Story Bank** (see page 28)

SKILLS Categorizing stories

ACTIVITY Categorizing newspaper story types

PREPARATION Write the following list on the board:

absurd	animal	embarrassing	enraging
funny	green	romantic	sad
sexy	sexist	silly	unbelievable
unjust	xenophobic	describing an accident	

PROCEDURE 1 Ask each student to choose one type of story to read from the list of story types on the board. Explain their meanings if necessary. Each student should keep their choice secret.

2 Distribute newspapers or your **Story Bank** and ask each student to scan the stories looking for good examples in their category. They should note down examples as they find them.

3 Ask students to work in groups of four or five and share their work.

COMMENTS This activity reveals the very wide range of story types to be found in the newspapers. It allows individual students to choose categories that interest them and determine whether each story they come across meets the necessary criteria for membership of the chosen category.

6.13 A story I associate with

LEVEL Intermediate and above, minimum class size 15

TIME 30 minutes

MATERIALS Story Bank (see page 28)

SKILLS Discussing text types

ACTIVITY Associating with newspaper stories

| PREPARATION | Display one story from your Story Bank for every four students in the class. |

PROCEDURE

1 Ask the students to read all the stories displayed on the wall. When they finish reading, they should return to their places and discuss the stories informally with neighbours. Once everyone is back in their place, move to the next Stage.

2 Ask each student to associate with a story. Which story do they feel closest to? Which one would they want to think about more deeply? Allow two or three minutes for this.

3 Ask the students to go to the story they associate with and discuss the reasons they are there with the other students who have associated with the same story.

COMMENTS

You can use this activity as the basis for forming groups to work on whatever you want to do next. Alternatively, you can give each group a task that relates to the story they have chosen.

6.14 A story I relate to

LEVEL

Upper-elementary and above

TIME

30–40 minutes

MATERIALS

Small objects (see Preparation), Story Bank (see page 28)

SKILLS

Matching memory and story

ACTIVITY

Relating newspaper stories to experience

PREPARATION

Take a large collection of small objects to class: flowers, leaves, bits of wrapping, food, sweets, buttons, rubbish from the floor of children's bedrooms, etc.

PROCEDURE

1 Ask the students to select an object and spend three to four minutes in silence associating memories with it. It often helps to makes notes in the mother tongue as the thought stream begins to flow.

2 Make your Story Bank available and ask the students to find a story that they can relate to one or more of their memories.

3 As the students each find a story, they should begin to circulate, taking their small object and story with them, and explain their choices to each other in English.

4 Stop the activity when the talk begins to die down. Encourage the students to take their small object and story away with them.

| VARIATION | If you have stories on the wall, perhaps as a result of an activity like 6.11, 'Classifying stories', you can use these instead of your Story Bank at Stage 2. |

COMMENTS If a painful memory is stirred and then picked up in a newspaper story, this can be a very powerful, or even upsetting, activity for the student concerned. Be ready for an emotional response. The value of the activity lies in the way that a target language newspaper story and a deeply felt memory can be united by the learner. It is a good idea to know something of your students' background before selecting this activity.

6.15 Reacting

LEVEL Upper-elementary and above

TIME 30–40 minutes

MATERIALS One newspaper for every five students

SKILLS Task reading

ACTIVITY Reacting to newspaper articles

PROCEDURE 1 Give out newspapers and ask each student to look for a story that makes them want to take some sort of action—write a letter, go and see someone, demonstrate, assassinate someone, or whatever. Allow up to 20 minutes.

2 Ask the students to work in pairs or threes and explain to each other which story made them feel the way they did.

COMMENTS 1 This activity works well with political news stories, so point any students who seem to be having difficulties in that direction.

2 Sometimes there is an outcome which is worth following up in a future lesson, such as writing an actual letter of protest or a letter seeking further information.

6.16 Brainstorming responses

LEVEL Intermediate and above

TIME 30 minutes

MATERIALS Story Bank (see page 28), blu-tack

SKILLS Reading for emotional response

ACTIVITY Responding authentically to newspaper stories

PREPARATION Display 20 stories from your Story Bank around the classroom.

PROCEDURE 1 Ask the students to come and write up on the board all the words they can think of that describe the reactions they might have to newspaper stories, such as annoyed, amused, disgusted, intrigued, surprised, etc. For example:

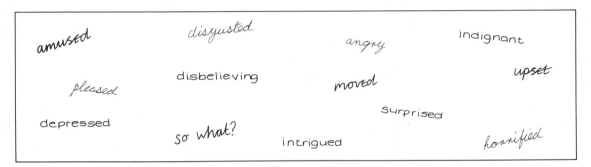

2 Once you have 25 words on the board, ask each student to tear a sheet of paper into 25 small pieces and write each word on a different one.

3 Distribute blu-tack and ask the students to read all the stories and stick the piece of paper on which the appropriate reaction is written on to the stories. (This will sometimes mean that they have not got any suitable piece of paper to attach, particularly if they get down to their last few.)

VARIATION If you have not got blu-tack available, you can always use glue, sellotape, or paper clips, or even simply place the reaction slips in an open envelope under each story.

COMMENTS This activity begins with 25 authentic responses to reading newspaper stories and then gives the reading task a real purpose, that of matching story and reaction.

6.17 Was it worth reading?

LEVEL	**Upper-elementary and above**
TIME	**30 minutes**
MATERIALS	**Ten newspaper articles, glue, coloured dots or felt pens**
SKILLS	**Reading evaluatively**
ACTIVITY	**Assessing the quality and value of newspaper articles**

PREPARATION

1 Choose 10 stories, features, and articles of various lengths on a variety of subjects and glue each to a large sheet of paper (A3 if possible). Display these on the walls.

2 If possible, obtain adhesive dots in four colours (say, blue, green, red, and yellow, but as long as they are all different it does not matter). You can get these from stationers and school librarians, who often use them for colour-coding books for subject, level of difficulty, etc. Otherwise each student will need a felt tip or coloured pencil in each colour.

PROCEDURE

1 Either hand out six or seven coloured dots in each colour to each student, or ask the students to prepare to use their own coloured pens.

2 Explain that each student will have a chance to read each story and after reading it must decide whether it was worth reading or not. They will indicate their judgements by sticking a coloured dot under the story (or making a coloured dot with a pen or pencil), for example:

Red—certainly worth reading
Yellow—worth reading
Green—not really worth reading
Blue—not worth reading at all

(Substitute the colours you have available.)

COMMENTS

The is an empowering activity in the sense that it makes the students the arbiters of quality. The results always *look* good. It is also interesting for the students to see where they are in a majority and where in a minority. Ultimately, the most relevant judgement about anything we read, in a newspaper or elsewhere, is whether it was worth reading.

6.18 Yuk

LEVEL	**Upper-intermediate and above**
TIME	**40–60 minutes**
MATERIALS	**Popular newspapers containing tasteless material, access to a photocopier**
SKILLS	**Identifying offensive writing**
ACTIVITY	**Discovering how tasteless popular journalism can be**

PREPARATION

Choose the five or six newspaper pages that contain the most tasteless stories and headlines that you can find. Make enough photocopies for each student to get one page.

PROCEDURE

1 Seat the students in a circle and hand out the photocopies. Make sure that each student has a different page from their neighbours. Allow reading time. Ask each student to cross out the most tasteless word, headline, picture, and whole story on the page.

2 Ask the students to exchange their pages with their neighbours and repeat Stage 1. This time they must choose a new most tasteless word, headline, picture, and whole story.

3 This stage may be repeated as many times (up to five or six) as seems appropriate.

4 Group students who have ended up with the same page and ask them to find anything pleasant left on their page to share with the class.

VARIATION

If you do not have access to a photocopier, this activity works equally well if you display half as many tasteless pages on the wall as you have students in the class. Each student should cross out their tasteless, word, headline, picture, and whole story on different pages.

COMMENTS

This activity can play an important part in conveying a realistic picture of popular English-speaking culture.

Acknowledgement
The idea of crossing out tasteless material is John Morgan's.

6.19 Affective language

LEVEL Intermediate and above

TIME 50–60 minutes

MATERIALS Three newspaper articles, glue, access to a photocopier (but see Variation)

SKILLS Recognizing affective language

ACTIVITY Discovering how newspapers play on emotions

PREPARATION Choose three very different items from the newspapers, such as a violent story, an advertisement, and a law report. Glue these items to a single large sheet of paper and make a copy for each student.

PROCEDURE 1 Distribute the photocopies and allow five minutes' reading time.

2 Explain that each student is going to list the affective language in the stories. Explain what you mean by 'affective': you are looking for language that provokes an emotional response of some kind. It may be that the language is violent, soothing, boring, irritating, too difficult, memory-evoking, warm, etc.

3 Ask the students to draw a box divided into nine squares in three rows of three.

4 Allow five more minutes' reading time while each student decides on their own three affective categories, one for each story, and labels their matrices as shown below.

	Violent	Sad	Boring
Story 1			
Story 2			
Story 3			

5 Each student now studies their three stories and enters every example of affective language they can find in the appropriate box. Allow 20 minutes.

	Violent	Sad	Boring
Story 1 'Ban on migrant cheats'	breakneck torture booted out persecution	refugees fleeing crisis-torn appeal	Ministers benefits fraud for years
Story 2 'Euromania haunts language of food'	polemic thought control	'wonder if he can please anyone'	Eurocrats designations regulation
Story 3 'Bible-basher'	punched row hits attack dragged kicked bruises	lovesick divorcee obsession	sentenced carrier bag gardener

6 Ask the students to work in groups of three and share their work.

VARIATION

If you do not have access to a photocopier, this activity is still possible. Here's how:

1 Distribute newspapers or your Story Bank (see page 28) and ask the students to work in threes. Each group should find three very different newspaper articles.

2 Follow Stages 2 and 3 above.

3 Follow Stages 4 and 5 above. Make sure that each student chooses their affective categories without consulting the others in the group.

4 Follow Stages 6 and 7 above.

COMMENTS

This activity brings into the open an aspect of language that is often suppressed in foreign language teaching. Yet it is an aspect we all intuitively respond to and is easily recognized by students.

Appendix

This appendix contains a brief list of some of the English-language newspapers either published or readily available in countries where English is not the first language of most people. This list is representative rather than exhaustive and is provided as an illustration of the wide availability of English-language newspapers even in countries where English is not the first language of the majority of the population—or even, in some cases, of any of the population.

Worldwide

Many British and American publications are available worldwide. These include newspapers such as the New York *Herald Tribune* and weeklies such as the *Guardian Weekly*. Some weekly journals such as *The Economist*, *Newsweek*, and *Time* also contain articles that are suitable for many of the exercises in this book.

Europe

It is possible to buy British newspapers in most countries in Europe. The New York *Herald Tribune* and the *Guardian* are both printed on the European mainland. Many of the most important national dailies (for example, *Le Monde* and *Die Zeit*) also print a weekly English-language supplement. There are also several locally produced English-language newspapers. Sometimes these contain materials written by non-native speakers and sometimes materials reprinted from British and American newspapers, as well as articles translated from other non-English major European newspapers. Well-known examples of this category of newspaper include the *Athens News* and the *Warsaw Voice*.

The Commonwealth

Many Commonwealth countries have English-language newspapers. Some of the best known are the *Botswana Daily News*; the *Gambia Weekly*; *Amrita Bazar Patrika*, the *Sunday Statesman*, the *Telegraph*, and the *Times of India* (India); the *Daily Nation*, *Kenya Times*, and the *Standard* (Kenya); the *Daily Times* (Malawi); the *Malay Mail*, *New Straits Times*, the *Star*, and the

New Sunday Times (Malaysia); the *Business Times*, *Daily Times*, the *Guardian*, the *Lagos Weekend*, the *National Concord*, and the *Sunday Times* (Nigeria); the *Pakistan Times*; the *Straits Times* (Singapore); the *Business Times* , *Daily News*, and *Sunday News* (Tanzania); the *New Vision* (Uganda); and the *Sunday Mail* (Zimbabwe).

Rest of the world

English-language newspapers are also readily found in many other countries where there has been a long contact with Britain. Good examples include the *Borneo Bulletin* (Brunei); *Gulf News* (Dubai); the *Hong Kong Standard* and the *South China Morning Post* (Hong Kong); the *Daily Gulf Times* (Qatar); *Arab News*, *Riyadh Daily*, and *Saudi Gazette* (Saudi Arabia).

In many other countries too there has been a long tradition of English language education, so that in Ethiopia, for example, you find the *Ethiopian Herald*. In yet other countries, the recognition of the status of English as a world language is reflected in local English-language newspapers. Good examples in this category include the *Asahi Evening News*, the *Daily Yomiuri*, the *Japan Times*, and the *Mainichi Daily News* (Japan); the *Korea Herald* and the *Korea Times* (South Korea); and the *China News* and *China Post* (Taiwan).

Even where there is no widely circulated English-language newspaper, there are often papers aimed at expatriates and tourists which can contain interesting articles.

The purpose of this appendix is to reinforce the point made in the Introduction (page 6) that English-language newspapers are a cheap, readily available source of contemporary, authentic written English. There is no reason to seek out newspapers originating in Britain or the USA for the vast majority of the exercises in this book—whatever is most readily available in your own country will do fine.

Periodicals

There are several weekly or monthly news magazines which can be subscribed to from all over the world, which contain articles which can be used for many of the activities in this book.

Subscription addresses of three follow:

Guardian Weekly
164 Deansgate, Manchester M60 2RR, England.

A digest of the week's news as reported in the *Guardian* newspaper.

Time magazine
Ottho Heldringstraat 5, 1000 AD Amsterdam, Netherlands.

No connection with *The Times* newspaper.

Newsweek
Key West, 53 Windsor Road, Slough, Berks SL1 2EH, England.

Bibliography

Abbott, J. 1981. *Meet the Press*. Cambridge: Cambridge University Press (out of print).

Abbs, B. and **I. Freebairn.** 1990. *Blueprint*. London: Longman.

Baddock, B. 1984. *Scoop*. Oxford: Pergamon.

Hamp-Lyons, L. and **B. Heasley.** 1987. *Study Writing*. Cambridge: Cambridge University Press.

Mercer, D. (ed.) 1992 (new edn). *Chronicle of the Twentieth Century*. London: Random Century.

Swan, M. 1975. *Inside Meaning*. Cambridge: Cambridge University Press.

Other titles in the Resource Books for Teachers series

CALL, by David Hardisty and Scott Windeatt – offers the teacher a bank of practical activities, based on communicative methodology, which make use of a variety of computer programs. (ISBN 0 19 437105 0)

Class Readers, by Jean Greenwood – is a comprehensive collection of activities offering practical advice and suggestions on how to exploit class readers to promote language and to develop both perceptive and literary skills. (ISBN 0 19 437103 4)

Classroom Dynamics, by Jill Hadfield – a practical book designed to help teachers establish and maintain a good working relationship with their classes, and so promote effective learning. It contains activities for ice-breaking, fostering self-confidence and group identity, and the end of term, plus a chapter on 'coping with crisis'. (ISBN 0 19 437147 6)

Conversation, by Rob Nolasco and Lois Arthur – the authors' approach is to examine what native speakers do when they 'make conversation', and then use this information as the basis for more than eighty activities. (ISBN 0 19 437096 8)

Drama, by Charlyn Wessels – used effectively, drama can change a roomful of strangers into a happy cohesive group and make the process of language learning a great deal more creative and enjoyable. (ISBN 0 19 437097 6)

Grammar Dictation, by Ruth Wajnryb – offers an innovative approach to the study of grammar in the language classroom. The procedure (sometimes called 'dictogloss') encourages student reconstruction of texts. (ISBN 0 19 437004 6)

Learner-based Teaching, by Colin Campbell and Hanna Kryszewska – is based on the principle that language practice activities should use the wealth of knowledge and experience that learners bring to the classroom. (ISBN 0 19 437163 8)

Literature, by Alan Maley and Alan Duff – is not a book on how to study literature, but on how to use it for language practice. The activities described can be used not only with the sample material provided, but also with other materials of the teacher's own choice. (ISBN 0 19 437094 1)

Music and Song, by Tim Murphey – contains ideas for using all types of music and song in the classroom in lively and interesting ways. It shows teachers how 'tuning in' to their students' musical tastes can increase motivation and tap a rich vein of resources. (ISBN 0 19 437055 0)

Project Work, by Diana L. Fried-Booth – a collection of full-scale projects of different kinds, lengths, and complexity is described in detail. The activities involved bridge the gap between the classroom and the outside world. (ISBN 0 19 437092 5)

Role Play, Gillian Porter Ladousse – encompasses an extremely varied collection to activities ranging from highly controlled conversations to improvised drama, and from simple dialogues to complex scenarios. (ISBN 0 19 437095 X)

Self-Access, by Susan Sheerin – is designed to help EFL and ESL teachers with the practicalities of setting up and managing self-access study facilities and so enable learning to take place independently of teaching. (ISBN 0 19 437099 2)

Translation, by Alan Duff – explores the role of translation in language learning and provides the teacher with a wide variety of translation activities from many different subject areas. No specialist knowledge or previous experience of translation is required. (ISBN 0 19 437104 2)

Video, by Richard Cooper, Mike Lavery, and Mario Rinvolucri – differs radically from other books on this topic in that it encourages students to control the interaction between camera and image, thus providing a wide range of communicative situations and activities. (ISBN 0 19 437102 6)

Vocabulary, by John Morgan and Mario Rinvolucri – emphasizes activities which encourage the students' own personal response, while facilitating exploration and extension of the language. This book will be of use to all teachers, including those in non-EFL classrooms. (ISBN 0 19 437091 7)

Writing, by Tricia Hedge – presents a range of writing tasks within a framework of current thinking on the process of writing. It discusses the different areas of writing ability and looks at ways in which classroom activities can help learners to develop these skills. (ISBN 0 19 437098 4)